Approaching Zanzibar

ALSO BY TINA HOWE

COASTAL DISTURBANCES: FOUR PLAYS

Museum

The Art of Dining

Painting Churches

Coastal Disturbances

Date Due

Approaching Zanzibar is supported, in part, by a grant from the New York State Council on the Arts.

TCG also gratefully acknowledges public funds from the National Endowment for the Arts, in addition to the generous support of the following foundations and corporations: Alcoa Foundation; Ameritech Foundation; ARCO Foundation; AT&T Foundation; Beatrice Foundation; Center for Arts Criticism; Citicorp/ Citibank; Common Wealth Fund; Consolidated Edison Company of New York; Eleanor Naylor Dana Charitable Trust; Dayton Hudson Foundation; Exxon Corporation; Ford Foundation; Jerome Foundation; Andrew W. Mellon Foundation; Metropolitan Life Foundation; National Broadcasting Company; New York Community Trust; New York Times Company Foundation; Pew Charitable Trusts; Philip Morris Companies; Scherman Foundation; Shell Oil Company Foundation; Shubert Foundation; Lila Wallace-Reader's Digest Fund; Xerox Foundation.

On the cover: Angela Goethals and Clayton Barclay Jones.
Photograph copyright © 1989 by Susan Cook.

Design and composition by The Sarabande Press

Howe, Tina.
    Approaching Zanzibar / Tina Howe.
    ISBN 1-55936-008-9
    I. Title.
PS3558.0894A85   1990
812'.54—dc20

FOR DARA

Approaching Zanzibar was first presented by Second Stage Theatre on April 8, 1989. The director was Carole Rothman. Scenic design was by Heidi Landesman, lighting design by Dennis Parichy, costume design by Susan Hilferty, and sound design by Gary and Timmy Harris. The cast was as follows:

WALLACE BLOSSOM	*Harris Yulin*
CHARLOTTE BLOSSOM	*Jane Alexander*
TURNER BLOSSOM	*Clayton Barclay Jones*
PONY BLOSSOM	*Angela Goethals*
RANDY WANDS	*Jamie Ross*
PALACE ST. JOHN	*Maggie Burke*
FLETCHER ST. JOHN	*Damien Jackson*
SCOTTY CHILDS	*Jamie Ross*
JOY CHILDS	*Aleta Mitchell*
AMY CHILDS	*Damien Jackson*
DALIA PAZ	*Aleta Mitchell*
OLIVIA CHILDS	*Bethel Leslie*
DR. SYBIL WREN	*Maggie Burke*

Approaching Zanzibar

CHARACTERS

WALLACE BLOSSOM, a composer, 49.

CHARLOTTE BLOSSOM, his wife, 45.

TURNER BLOSSOM, their son, a prodigy, 12.

PONY BLOSSOM, their nearsighted daughter, 9.

RANDY WANDS, a new father, 43.

PALACE ST. JOHN, a hearty grandmother, 63.

FLETCHER ST. JOHN, her deaf grandson, 11.

SCOTTY CHILDS, Charlotte's brother, a landscape architect, 48.

JOY CHILDS, his new wife, a TV newscaster who's black and seven months pregnant, 28.

AMY CHILDS, Scotty's athletic daughter, played by a boy, 11.

DALIA PAZ, Olivia's Mexican nurse, 28.

OLIVIA CHILDS, Charlotte's aunt, an eminent site-specific artist, 81.

DR. SYBIL WREN, her doctor, with a severe limp, 60s.

Actors are encouraged to double in the supporting roles.

PLAYWRIGHT'S NOTE

This is a challenging play to design since it covers over two thousand miles of scenic splendor. I imagined the set being made of fabric because fabric is lightweight and versatile. It can change shape and context in the twinkling of an eye. Also, it's Olivia's medium. But an inspired designer can work wonders with many materials — screens, rugs, ladders, slide projections — so don't feel bound by my limited imagination.

Act One

SCENE 1

The Blossoms are driving towards Falling Waters, West Virginia, in a station wagon. It's the first week of August, around ten in the evening. Wally's at the wheel and Charlotte sits next to him. Turner and Pony are piled in the back along with all their gear. Pony wears glasses. They're all singing "Ninety-nine Bottles of Beer on the Wall" with flagging energy.

ALL:

Forty-four bottles of beer on the wall,
Forty-four bottles of beer,
If one of those bottles should happen to fall,
Forty-three bottles of beer on the wall.

Forty-three bottles of beer on the wall,

Forty-three bottles of beer,
If one of those bottles should happen to fall,
Forty-two bottles of beer on the wall.

Forty-two bottles of beer on the wall,
Forty-two bottles of beer,
If one of those bottles should happen to fall,
Forty-one bottles of beer on the wall . . .

CHARLOTTE: STOP . . . STOP . . . I CAN'T TAKE IT
ANYMORE!

WALLY, TURNER AND PONY:
Forty-one bottles of beer on the wall,
Forty-one bottles of beer,
If one of those bottles should happen to fall,
Forty bottles of beer on the wall.

CHARLOTTE: Pleeeease?

TURNER AND PONY (*Softly*):
Forty bottles of beer on the wall,
Forty bottles of beer,
If one of those bottles should happen to fall . . .

WALLY: Your mother asked you to stop.

TURNER AND PONY (*Softer*):
Thirty-nine bottles of beer on the wall.

Thirty-nine bottles of beer on the wall,
Thirty-nine bottles of beer,
If one of those bottles should happen to fall . . .

CHARLOTTE: Kids . . . ?!

TURNER AND PONY (*Barely audible*):
Thirty-eight bottles of beer on the wall . . .

WALLY: IF YOU DON'T STOP RIGHT THIS

MINUTE, I'M PULLING OVER TO THE SIDE
OF THE ROAD!

*They keep humming. The sound of screeching brakes as
Wally veers over to the side of the road. They all lean to
the right.*

CHARLOTTE: LOOK   TURNER AND PONY: We
OUT, LOOK OUT!   stopped, we stopped!

*A silence. Wally straightens the wheel and eases back onto
the road.*

WALLY: Thank you.

Charlotte sighs deeply. Silence as Wally drives.

PONY: Are we there yet?

WALLY: We just started, for Christsakes! We have two
thousand more miles to go!

CHARLOTTE: Why do they always have to push us to the
breaking point? Why . . .? It's not fair.

Pause.

WALLY (*Suddenly whirls around, glaring at the
kids*): Answer her! WHY DO YOU ALWAYS
HAVE TO PUSH US TO THE BREAKING
POINT, HUH . . .? HUH . . .?!

PONY: I didn't do anything.

TURNER: Don't look at me. Pony was the one who—

CHARLOTTE: WALLY, EYES ON THE ROAD, PLEASE!

PONY: Right, right, it's always *my* fault.

WALLY (*Turning back towards the road*): Sorry, sorry . . .

TURNER *(To Pony)*: You were the one who kept singing.

PONY: You were singing too.

CHARLOTTE *(To Wally)*: You're already breaking the speed limit as it is.

TURNER *(To Pony)*: That's not true.

WALLY *(To Charlotte)*: Are you complaining about the way I'm driving?

TURNER *(To Pony)*: I stopped when Dad asked me to.

PONY: You did not!

TURNER: I did so!

PONY: Did not!

TURNER: Did so!

WALLY *(To Charlotte)*: Hello . . .?

PONY: Did not!

Faster and faster.

TURNER: Did so!

PONY: Did not!

TURNER: Did so!

CHARLOTTE *(To Wally)*: I just wish you wouldn't go so fast.

PONY: Did not, did not, did NOT!

WALLY: Since when is sixty-five fast?

TURNER *(Shoving Pony)*: DID SO!

PONY: OW . . . OW . . . TURNER PUSHED ME!

CHARLOTTE: The speed limit is fifty-five.

WALLY: Would you like to drive?

Pony bites Turner's arm.

TURNER *(Leaping out of his seat)*: YIIIIII! PONY BIT ME!

CHARLOTTE: All I said was: you're breaking the speed

limit. *(Turning around)* KIDS, PLEASE . . . ?!

WALLY: I happen to be a very safe driver.

Turner gives Pony a noogie.

PONY *(Leaping out of her seat)*: OW, OW . . . TURNER GAVE ME A NOOGIE, TURNER GAVE ME A NOOGIE!

They start wrestling.

PONY: I'm going to get you, Turner. Hold still! Will you hold still?! Turrrrner . . . ?!	TURNER: Oh . . . so you want to fight do you . . . ? All right, Pony . . . say your prayers!

The wrestling gets more ferocious.

CHARLOTTE *(Whirling around)*: KIDS, WE ASKED YOU TO BEHAVE!

WALLY *(Also whirling around)*: ALL RIGHT, WHAT'S GOING ON BACK THERE?

CHARLOTTE *(Grabbing the wheel)*: LOOK OUT, LOOK OUT!

They all veer to one side as the tires squeal.

WALLY *(Grabbing it back)*: GIVE ME THAT WHEEL!

They veer to the other side.

CHARLOTTE: WALLY, WE ALMOST WENT OFF THE ROAD!

The kids keep slugging each other.

WALLY: JESUS CHRIST, CHARLOTTE . . .

CHARLOTTE: What are you trying to do . . . ? *Kill* us?

WALLY: . . . YOU DON'T GRAB THE STEERING WHEEL OUT OF SOMEONE'S HANDS!

CHARLOTTE: We were going off the road!

PONY: I hate you, I hate you, I hate you, I hate you, I hate you, I hate you, I hate you —

TURNER: If you hurt my hands, I'll smash you. I really mean it, I'll smash you!

Wally pulls over to the side of the road and slams on the brakes. Everyone lurches forward and then back.

CHARLOTTE: Wally, what are you . . . ?

WALLY: *All right, that's it! That's it!*

A horrible silence.

WALLY (*Calm and collected*): I can take a hint. If you don't like the way I'm driving, *you* drive! (*He gets out of the car, slams his door and marches over to the passenger side*)

CHARLOTTE: Wally . . . ?!

He opens the door and pushes Charlotte over.

CHARLOTTE: Wally, what are you . . . ?

WALLY: Come on, move over, move over!

CHARLOTTE: *Wallace . . . ?!*

WALLY: I said . . . MOVE! (*He slams the door closed*)

CHARLOTTE: I didn't say I wanted to drive.

WALLY: Well, someone's got to drive if we want to make it to Rushing Rivers or wherever the hell it is . . .

CHARLOTTE: Hey, hey, *you* were the one who took the wrong turn off 81 . . .

WALLY: So now that's my fault too.

CHARLOTTE: And it's not Rushing Rivers, it's *Falling Waters*!

WALLY: Why we had to stop at Hershey, Pennsylvania, I'll never understand.

CHARLOTTE: Come on, you loved every minute of it!

WALLY: At the rate we're going, the campsite will be filled and we'll have to stay in a motel.

CHARLOTTE: Who had to go back in line a second time to watch the Chocolate Kisses being poured and wrapped, hmmmm?

WALLY: It's so typical. Our first day on the road and we'll have to stay in a motel! Pay a hundred and fifty bucks to sleep in some gummy room with a broken air conditioner . . . !

CHARLOTTE: We won't have to stay in a motel.

WALLY: If you'd been looking at the map instead of the goddamned speedometer all the time, I wouldn't have taken that turn!

CHARLOTTE: Okay, okay . . .

Pause.

CHARLOTTE: I just hate it when you speed. Especially with the kids in the car. It's just asking for trouble!	WALLY: I don't believe we're doing this . . . . *Driving* to New Mexico. How did you ever talk me into it?

Pause.

CHARLOTTE: If I hadn't grabbed the wheel, we'd all be lying dead in a ditch!	WALLY: Do you know how many more states we have to go through . . . ?

Pause.

CHARLOTTE: Is that how you want to start our vacation? All being piled into body bags at the side of the road?

WALLY: . . . Virginia, North Carolina, Tennessee, Alabama . . .

CHARLOTTE: We're not going anywhere *near* Alabama!

WALLY: Kentucky, Missouri, Arkansas, Oklahoma . . .

CHARLOTTE: She's dying, honey.

WALLY: There are about a hundred and fifty states between New York and New Mexico.

CHARLOTTE: I want to say good-bye.

WALLY: The airplane was invented for a reason, you know.

PONY: Mommy . . . ?

WALLY: Texas alone is the size of China.

CHARLOTTE: But I don't fly.

WALLY: Why do you have to take it out on us?

CHARLOTTE: Turner's never played for her. I want her to hear him.

PONY: Mommy . . . ?

WALLY: It'll take us seventy-five years to get there.

CHARLOTTE *(Opening her window)*: God, it's hot in here!

WALLY: We'll all be in walkers!

CHARLOTTE: Who's always complaining that we never take a vacation?

PONY: *Mommy* . . . ?

WALLY *(Putting on a creaky old voice)*: "Well, hi there Livvie, we finally made it! That *is* you, isn't it Liv? I don't see so good anymore."

PONY: Mommy, what's Livvie dying of?

TURNER: God Pony . . . !

WALLY (*Still playing aged*): "Hey there, Char, want to pass me my ear trumpet? I don't hear so good neither."

CHARLOTTE: We'll finally get to see the country . . . swim in freshwater streams, camp out under the stars . . . *go fly-fishing!*

WALLY: Well, at least I convinced you to leave Spit and Wheat Germ behind in a kennel.

PONY: Oh Spit . . . !

TURNER: Spitty, Spitty, Spit!

PONY: I MISS SPIT!

CHARLOTTE: We're going to have a great time! I can feel it!

PONY: I MISS SPIT, I MISS SPIT, I MISS SPIT, I MISS SPIT, I MISS SPIT . . . !	TURNER: SPITTY, SPITTY SPIT! SPITTY, SPITTY SPIT! SPITTY, SPITTY SPIT . . . !

They start barking.

CHARLOTTE: We'll get to spend some time with Scotty and Joy. We haven't seen them since the wedding. (*Turning around*) Remember Joy, kids?

WALLY: She is one classy lady. I don't know how Scotty ever nabbed her.

CHARLOTTE (*To the kids*): Come on, quiet down.

WALLY (*As a rallying cry*): We'll get to see Amy again!

CHARLOTTE (*Groaning*): Please!

Pony and Turner are now baying, yelping, panting and making other assorted canine sounds.

CHARLOTTE (*Whirling around*): KIDS, PLEASE! DADDY AND I ARE TRYING TO HAVE A CONVERSATION!

WALLY (*Likewise*): JESUS CHRIST GUYS, WILL YOU PIPE DOWN? THIS ISN'T A KENNEL!

Silence.

CHARLOTTE: God . . . !

WALLY: Give us a break!

CHARLOTTE: I mean, after a while . . .

Silence.

PONY (*In a tiny voice*): Mommy . . . ?

WALLY: There *are* other people in the car, you know.

CHARLOTTE: Daddy and I have *some* rights . . .

Silence.

WALLY (*To Charlotte*): So, are we going to sit here all night, or what?

PONY: Mommy . . . ?

CHARLOTTE: Oh right, right. Sorry. (*She swings back onto the road*)

TURNER: Where are we, anyway?

PONY: Mommy . . . ?

WALLY: *Who knows!*

PONY: I have to pee.

TURNER: You just went fifteen minutes ago.

CHARLOTTE: Why didn't you say something when we were stopped? (*Opening her window wider*) God, I'm burning up!

WALLY: So guys, is everyone ready for . . . *(Trumpet-fanfare sound)* Gamey Amy?!

CHARLOTTE *(Laughing)*: Oh no!   TURNER: Spare me!   PONY: She's so weird . . . !

WALLY: Boy wonder of the western world!

CHARLOTTE *(Trying not to laugh)*: Come on, don't be mean.

PONY: Mommy . . . ?

WALLY: The only eight-year-old girl I know who can throw a shotput fifty yards.

CHARLOTTE: Honey, she's eleven!

WALLY: And already shaving! *(He mimes using an electric razor)*

PONY: Mommy?

Turner joins Wally shaving.

CHARLOTTE *(Trying not to laugh)*: Come on, guys!

PONY: I have to pee, I have to pee!

WALLY: Charlotte, the girl's got sideburns and a moustache!

PONY: EWWWWWWW!   TURNER: Gross, gross!

CHARLOTTE: She's just very athletic. Look at her mother.

WALLY: That's a marriage I'll never understand. Your brother and Inge Trim . . .

CHARLOTTE: She was blonde, Swedish and a world-class track star.

TURNER: How many Olympic medals has she won?

WALLY: About three hundred. The woman lives to compete. I've never seen anything like it. *(To the kids)* She had Amy running a four-minute mile by the time she was seven.

CHARLOTTE: Honey . . . ?!

WALLY: And remember that craze with pole vaulting? Amy would start tearing up the driveway with this special broomstick and then BOIIIIINGGGGG . . . she'd suddenly be flying over the family car!

CHARLOTTE: *Wally . . . ?!*

WALLY: Inge Trim . . . . She had calves like a weightlifter.

PONY: I like Joy better.

CHARLOTTE: We all like Joy better. Scotty should have married her in the first place.

PONY: She's so beautiful.

CHARLOTTE: And *kind* . . . !

WALLY: She's also the first black newscaster in Oklahoma City, which is no small feat.

CHARLOTTE: She's wonderful. Amy adores her.

WALLY: Poor Amy.

CHARLOTTE: Poor Amy!

WALLY: Where was it she just won that big hang-gliding contest . . . ? Colorado? Wyoming? Arizona? No, wait, I remember, it was in Salt Lake City.

TURNER: Hey, let's play Geography again!

PONY (*Clapping her hands*): Geography, Geography, Geography!

CHARLOTTE: Oh, not again!

WALLY: Great idea!

PONY AND TURNER: Geography, Geography, Geography!

WALLY: Alabama!

TURNER: Arkansas! That ends in S, Pone.

PONY: I know, I know . . . . South Dakota!

TURNER: Mom . . . ?

WALLY: It's your turn, Char.

CHARLOTTE (*Opening her window more*): Sorry, sorry, I
    need more air.

TURNER: We're waiting . . .

CHARLOTTE (*Fanning herself as she drives*): Okay, okay . . .
    what did you say?

WALLY, TURNER AND PONY: SOUTH DAKOTA!

CHARLOTTE (*Recoils from the blast*): Arizona!

WALLY: Annapolis!

TURNER: Salem!

PONY: Mississippi!

WALLY: Islip!

TURNER: Islip? Where's Islip?

WALLY AND CHARLOTTE: Long Island.

WALLY: Go on Turner. You start with P.

TURNER: Um . . . Princeton!

Faster and faster.

PONY: New Mexico!

CHARLOTTE: Ohio!

WALLY: Oklahoma!

TURNER: Atlanta!

PONY: Alabama!

TURNER: Daddy already said Alabama. You're out, you're
    out.

WALLY AND CHARLOTTE: You're out, you're out!

PONY: No fair, no fair!

TURNER: Pony's out.

WALLY AND CHARLOTTE (*With an edge*): Pony's out,
    Pony's out!

PONY (*Near tears*): No fair, I'm always out first. It's not fair.

SCENE 2

Luray, Virginia, two days and 134 miles later. It's eight in the morning and pouring rain. The Blossoms are huddled around the door of their tent in their pajamas, glumly staring out.

WALLY: Well, there goes our hike up White Oak Canyon Trail.

CHARLOTTE: Just our luck!

PONY (*Yelling out at it*): LOUSY STINKY RAIN!

TURNER (*Leaning out the door, with his hands out, impressed*): Whoa, look at it come down!

CHARLOTTE (*Pulling Turner back in*): Get back in here, you'll get soaked!

WALLY: Well, at least it stopped thundering and lightning.

A great crash of thunder and lightning shivers around them.

PONY: HELP . . .   TURNER: FAR OUT!
  HELP . . . !

CHARLOTTE (*Terrified, drags them away from the door*): LOOK OUT, LOOK OUT!

WALLY: Me and my big mouth!

CHARLOTTE (*Drops to the floor with her arms over her head*): Quick, down on the floor.

TURNER: Mom . . . ?

WALLY: Take it easy, Charlotte.

CHARLOTTE (*Rocking back and forth*): Our Father who art in Heaven, hallowed be thy name. Thy kingdom come, thy will be done on earth as it is in Heaven. Give us this day our daily bread . . .

TURNER: It was just a little thunder.

PONY (*Suddenly all smiles*): That was neat!

They stare at Charlotte as she continues to pray.

WALLY (*Goes over to Charlotte, offering her his hand*): Honey . . . ?

CHARLOTTE (*Being pulled to her feet*): Sorry, sorry. You know me and thunderstorms . . .

TURNER: Did you know that fireflies are immune to lightning? It just bounces right off them.

WALLY: Where did you hear that?

TURNER: Salvatore Argenti told me.

CHARLOTTE: God, it looks as if a bomb went off in here!

WALLY: Salvatore Argenti . . .?

CHARLOTTE: Come on guys, what do you say we start straightening up? (*She begins folding a brightly woven blanket*)

TURNER: He told me during our master class last month.

CHARLOTTE: Wal, want to give me a hand with this?

WALLY: He did? Where was I? (*He helps Charlotte fold*) This is really beautiful. You know you're a damned good weaver.

CHARLOTTE: Why, thank you.

WALLY: I wish you'd take it more seriously.

CHARLOTTE: Honey, I don't have time anymore what with the kids . . .

TURNER: He said that because they're already filled with light, they can never be hurt by it. It's the same with electric eels . . .

CHARLOTTE *(Voice lowered)*: He was using it as a metaphor about prodigies.

WALLY: Right, right, I remember.

TURNER: They can't be electrocuted.

Pony runs to a corner of the tent and stands on her head.

CHARLOTTE: Too much talent never destroyed anyone.

PONY: HEY, EVERYBODY LOOK AT ME!

TURNER: Pony, one of these days your brains are going to fall out. They're just going to start oozing out your ears.

WALLY *(Starts folding a sleeping bag)*: It's the goddamned world that mucks everything up. You're plodding along writing your trios and suites and . . . FOOM . . .

TURNER: Blub, blub, blub . . . *(He keeps it up)*

WALLY: . . . suddenly the melodies elude you.

PONY: It's so neat seeing everything upside down.

WALLY: A great silence descends . . .

CHARLOTTE *(Also folding a bag)*: Careful Pony, or you'll break your glasses again. Come on kids, pitch in.

WALLY: Thank God for teaching.

PONY: Your mouths look so funny when you talk . . . *(She exaggerates her jaw movements)* Ba ba ba ba ba ba ba . . . *(She keeps it up)*

WALLY *(Moving on to the kids' sleeping bags)*: So . . . how did everybody sleep last night?

CHARLOTTE: Don't ask. *(Mopping her brow)* God, it's hot in here!

PONY: You look like marionettes . . . . Ba ba ba ba
    ba . . .

CHARLOTTE *(To Wally)*: I heard the baby again.

WALLY: Honey, it's just a dream.

PONY: Come on Turn, join me. It's so fun. Ba ba ba
    ba . . .

TURNER: Yeah . . . ? *(He stands on his head next to her)*

CHARLOTTE: Wally, I heard it!

WALLY: People don't abandon babies in the wilderness.
    They leave them in bus terminals or movie theaters.

CHARLOTTE: It was sobbing and sobbing as if its little
    heart would break.

TURNER: This *is* neat! *(Imitating them)* Ba ba ba ba ba . . .

CHARLOTTE: I almost went out to look for him.

WALLY: Him? How do you know it's a boy?

CHARLOTTE: Because I saw him.

WALLY: You *saw* him? When did you see him?

CHARLOTTE: The night before last.

WALLY: But we were in West Virginia.

Turner and Pony flop back down to their feet to listen.

CHARLOTTE: It's weird, he's been following us I
    finally went out and looked for him last night. I
    found him nestled in a bed of dandelions under a
    hawthorn bush . . . . He's a sort of changeling with
    bright blue eyes and berries in his hair. He has
    pointed ears and the rosiest cheeks you've ever seen.
    They look like little hearts pulsing under his
    skin . . . . I know, I know, I sound like a lunatic,
    but I've seen him. He smells like cinnamon and has
    this wonderful rippling laugh like a grown man . . .

TURNER *(Suddenly freezing)*: SSSSHHHHHHHH!

CHARLOTTE *(In a whisper)*: What is it?

TURNER: Nobody move.

CHARLOTTE: *Turner . . . ?!*

TURNER: Listen.

Dead silence.

CHARLOTTE *(In a whisper)*: I don't hear anything.

WALLY: Neither do I.

TURNER: Shhhhh! Quiet!

Pony starts to whimper in fear.

WALLY, CHARLOTTE AND TURNER
(Whispered): Pony . . . !

She stops. Dead silence.

TURNER *(Barely audible)*: There it is again.

WALLY: *What?*

TURNER: The earth is turning.

WALLY: What are you talking about?

TURNER: Shhhh!

Silence.

PONY *(In a whisper)*: I hear it.

WALLY: It's something outside the tent.

PONY *(Barely audible)*: It's bears. Big. Black. Bears!

WALLY: An animal of some kind.

CHARLOTTE: Oh, I hear it too!

WALLY, TURNER AND PONY *(To Charlotte)*: SSHHHHHH!

Silence.

TURNER: It's the humming of the spheres . . .

WALLY: Raccoons!

CHARLOTTE (*In a whisper*): It's someone with a limp.

Pony whimpers.

TURNER: . . . suns and planets moving through
space . . .

CHARLOTTE: They're coming closer!

PONY (*Clinging to Charlotte*): It's the boogeyman, it's the
boogeyman!

WALLY (*Prepared for the worst*): Stand back!

TURNER (*Transported*): It sounds like people singing . . .

*They freeze as we all hear a wondrous faraway sound.
Charlotte gasps.*

PONY: I hear it, I hear it!

CHARLOTTE (*Enchanted*): Oh, Turner . . .

TURNER: What did I tell you?

WALLY: Only you . . .

CHARLOTTE (*Murmuring*): Turner, Turner . . .

SCENE 3

*The Blossoms have just reached a spectacular lookout high
up in the Blue Ridge Mountains. It's a perfect afternoon
one day and 122 miles later. Standing with them are
Randy Wands with his three-week-old baby, William,
strapped to his chest. They're all gazing at the view, frozen
with awe. Nothing happens for several moments.*

Charlotte takes a deep breath. Wally focuses his camera.

Turner beats his chest. Pony plucks a nearby wildflower.
Silence.

CHARLOTTE: Oh Wally . . .

Turner yodels like an ape.

WALLY (*Snaps his picture*): Got it!
RANDY (*Turning so William can see the view*): Well
  William, what do you think?

Pony eats the flower.

WALLY: The Blue Ridge Mountains . . .
CHARLOTTE: Look . . . ! (*She sighs deeply*)
RANDY (*To William*): Pretty impressive, eh what?
WALLY: . . . one of the oldest land areas on earth.

Turner beats his chest and yodels again. Pony joins him.

WALLY: We're talking over 400 million years here. The
  Fertile Crescent was still underwater.
RANDY (*To the others*): This is his first time up here.
CHARLOTTE: You can see forever.
RANDY: You think this is something, you ought to see it
  after a snowfall. It's like standing on top of the
  North Pole. White . . . white . . . white!
CHARLOTTE (*Hands over her ears*): Kids, please?!

Turner and Pony stop.

RANDY: Forget the sledding . . . ! My wife and I have
  already bought him one of those aluminum numbers
  that looks like a satellite dish. Woooosh! I can't wait!
  My daddy used to bring me up here when *I* was

little. We'd ease down on that old Flexible Flyer and go belly whopping all the way to Nashville and back. My mother'd have to pry us off with a crowbar . . . and then summers we'd come up here with chili dogs and soda and play our harmonicas. He was good, he was real good. When he got going, the bears would come popping out of those bushes and start stomping their feet like there was no tomorrow . . . ! *(He pulls out a harmonica and plays a few lively measures)*

PONY: My brother plays too.

RANDY: No kidding?

PONY: He's a prodigy. His name is Turner Blossom.

TURNER: *Pony . . . ?!*

WALLY: Now Pony . . .

RANDY *(Handing him the harmonica)*: Well, come on, let's hear you do your stuff!

TURNER: I play the guitar.

PONY *(More and more braggy)*: The classical guitar. He's been touched by God. *(She plucks another wildflower and starts eating the petals)*

TURNER *(Blazing with embarrassment)*: Pony?!

WALLY *(To Pony)*: Easy honey . . . and take that flower out of your mouth. What is this with suddenly eating flowers all the time?

PONY *(She quickly swallows it)*: He goes to Juilliard and everything.

TURNER *(To Pony)*: Will you stop it?

PONY: He's even played with symphony orchestras.

TURNER *(Lunging after her)*: I'm going to kill her!

WALLY *(Trying to restrain him)*: Easy, easy . . .

PONY: My daddy's a composer. His name is Wallace
    Blossom.

WALLY: All right Pony, cool it.

PONY: He teaches at Juilliard.

RANDY: Well, you sound like quite a family.

PONY: He wrote *The Atlantic Suite.*

   A pause.

RANDY *(Trying to place it)*: *The Atlantic Suite* . . . ?

PONY *(Eager)*: Have you heard it?

WALLY: Pony, enough is enough!

PONY: It's played all over the world.

WALLY: Rio and Tokyo are hardly the whole world, and
    that was three years ago.

CHARLOTTE *(To Wally)*: Now, now . . .

RANDY: Well, William, it looks as if we've stumbled into
    some pretty fancy company here.

   Charlotte sneaks a look at William.

WALLY: No, make it four . . . four and a half, to be
    more accurate. And at the rate I'm going, it'll be
    twenty years before I come up with something else.
    (He goes and stands by himself)

CHARLOTTE: Wally . . . ?

RANDY: So, where are you folks from?

CHARLOTTE: Hastings, New York. *(To Wally)* Honey . . . ?

RANDY: Say, you wouldn't know Panda Orenstein, would
    you?

CHARLOTTE: Panda Orenstein . . . ?

RANDY: Tall, red hair . . . she drives a green pickup
    truck . . . ?

CHARLOTTE: I know a Panda Vogel, but not a Panda
Orenstein. Sorry.

RANDY: Great legs! I was real sweet on her once.
Whoooie, that Panda Orenstein was something else!
(Pause) So, where are you heading?

CHARLOTTE: Taos, New Mexico. *(She glances at William
again)*

RANDY: *New Mexico?!*

CHARLOTTE: We're driving across the country to visit my
aunt.

PONY: Olivia Childs, the famous artist who builds fabric
mounds and circles in the desert.

TURNER *(Turning his back)*: I don't know her.

RANDY *(To Charlotte)*: Your aunt is Olivia Childs . . . ?
(To William) Did you hear that William, these people
are related to Olivia Childs.

PONY: She just finished a circle of 1,000 kites.

RANDY: Right, right, I read about it in the paper.
What's it called . . . ?

CHARLOTTE AND PONY: "Ring of Prayer."

RANDY: That's right, "Ring of Prayer" . . . a giant circle
of snow-white kites.

WALLY *(Rejoining them with his camera)*: Come on guys, I
want to take a picture of you up here.

RANDY: How does she come up with that stuff? Deco-
rating the desert with sails and parachutes and
wedding veils . . . ?

CHARLOTTE: Her pieces mark sacred Indian sites.

RANDY: But don't they blow away?

CHARLOTTE: That's the whole point—the risk of losing it
all before the photographers get airborne. Her work

celebrates its vulnerability to nature . . . . Prayer is eternal, but our shrines are made of air.

WALLY (*Waving at his family*): Scrunch together!

CHARLOTTE (*Gazes at sleeping William and whispers*): What a beautiful baby.

RANDY: Why thank you.

CHARLOTTE (*Touching his face*): His *skin* . . . !

WALLY (*Motioning to Charlotte*): Come on guys, let's have a little cooperation here.

CHARLOTTE (*To Randy*): How old is he?

RANDY: Just three weeks.

WALLY: *Sweetheart* . . . ?

CHARLOTTE: Can't you see I'm involved in something else?

WALLY: If we want photographs of this trip, someone's got to take them.

CHARLOTTE (*To Wally*): All right, all right. Come on kids, Daddy wants to take a picture of us.

RANDY: Well, I hope you have a great time with that aunt of yours. She sounds like quite a woman.

PONY: She's dying of cancer.

CHARLOTTE: *Pony* . . . ?!

RANDY: I'm so sorry, that's the worst . . .

CHARLOTTE (*Pulling the kids closer*): Tell me about it.

WALLY (*Shaking his head*): Please!

RANDY: . . . the worst!

Charlotte heaves a deep sigh. Palace St. John, a hearty woman in her sixties, and Fletcher, her deaf grandson, join them and gaze out at the view.

CHARLOTTE (*Nodding towards Wally*): He lost both his parents last year. Both!

PONY: She may not even be alive when we get there.

RANDY: To every thing there is a season, and a time to every purpose under heaven.

An uncomfortable silence.

RANDY *(Undaunted)*: A time to be born, and a time to die, a time to plant and a time to pluck up that which is planted . . .

WALLY: Okay guys, say "cheese."

They mournfully say "cheese."

WALLY: Come on, smile!

They try again, forced.

CHARLOTTE: Honestly dear, your sense of timing . . . !

Fletcher approaches Wally and reaches for his camera with authority.

PALACE: Let my grandson take it so you can be in it too. He's a whiz with cameras.

WALLY: Yeah? *(He hands it to him)* Well, thanks a lot.

Charlotte suddenly rips open her blouse and starts fanning herself.

CHARLOTTE: God, it's hot up here!

WALLY: Charlotte . . . ?

TURNER: Mom . . . ?!

Fletcher snaps away.

RANDY: Take it off, take it off!

WALLY: . . . what *are* you doing?

RANDY (*Laughing*): I love it, I love it!

CHARLOTTE (*Fanning herself with both hands*): Well, I guess these are the hot flashes my doctor was warning me about, though I still say I'm much too young to be going through this.

WALLY (*Indicating she's exposed*): Honey . . . ?

CHARLOTTE (*Quickly buttons herself back up, laughing*): Oh, sorry, sorry . . . (*To Fletcher*) Sorry.

Fletcher starts arranging them into a classic family portrait.

WALLY (*Hushed*): She's right, the boy *is* good!

PONY: This is so fun!

WALLY (*To Charlotte*): Now we'll really have something to show for this crazy escapade of ours.

Fletcher suddenly pulls Pony away from the others and places her in her own special row in front. He then snaps the picture and hands the camera back to Wally.

WALLY: Thanks a lot, that was terrific.

CHARLOTTE: Yes, you're really wonderful. Say thank you, kids.

TURNER: Thank you.

PONY: More, more!

CHARLOTTE: Now Pony.

PONY (*Pulling on Fletcher*): More, more . . . !

PALACE (*Hugging him*): Yes, Fletcher has quite an eye . . .

RANDY: Well, William, we better head back home or Mom and the twins will think we've run away to join the circus.

CHARLOTTE (*Gazing at William again*): Kids, you've got to come see this baby, he's awake now.

PONY (*Joining her*): Ohhh, he's so cute!

PALACE: He's just beautiful.

RANDY: Here, let's get you out of this thing so everyone can get a good look at you.

WALLY (*Chucking William under the chin*): Well hi there, bright eyes, what's happening?

CHARLOTTE: He's precious.

RANDY: Say thank you, William.

CHARLOTTE: Just precious!

PONY: Look at his fingers, they're like candy corns.

WALLY (*Talking baby talk and making faces*): Is someone trying to smile, hmmm? Yes, yes, yes . . . ! (*He makes more faces*)

RANDY: Well William, is everyone admiring you?

WALLY: Yes! You can do it. Let's see those rosy gums . . .

RANDY (*Lowering his head into William*): Willie, Willie, Willie! (*He makes loud buffling noises into the baby's stomach*)

WALLY: YES! LITTLE BABY. Ba ba ba ba ba! Little cheeks! What have you got in there . . . ? Tennis balls?

TURNER (*Pulling on Wally's sleeve*): Easy, Dad, easy . . .

WALLY (*Recovering*): Sorry, sorry . . .

CHARLOTTE: He really is spectacular.

PONY: Aren't you afraid he's going to break?

PALACE: Babies are very strong.

FLETCHER (*Signs to Palace*): What day was he born?

PONY: *He's deaf . . . ?!*

The Blossoms and Randy stare open-mouthed at Fletcher.

CHARLOTTE AND WALLY *(Catching themselves, to Pony)*: Shhhhh!
PONY *(In a whisper)*: Sorry, sorry . . .
CHARLOTTE *(Quietly)*: Honestly, Pony!

An awkward silence.

PALACE: He wants to know when his birthday was.
RANDY *(Too loud)*: JULY 7TH!
PALACE *(Signs back to Fletcher)*: July 7th.
CHARLOTTE: July 7th? That's Livvie's birthday! *(To Randy)* Olivia Childs. She just turned eighty-one. Did you hear that Wally? The baby was born on the same day as Livvie. What a coincidence!
FLETCHER *(Signs to Palace)*: What time was he born?
PALACE: He wants to know what time he was born.
RANDY: 6:13 A.M. ELEVEN POUNDS, THREE OUNCES.
PALACE *(To Randy)*: You don't have to yell, he can't hear you anyway.
RANDY *(Mortified)*: Right, right . . . *(To Fletcher)* Sorry about that.
PALACE *(Signs to Fletcher)*: 6:13 A.M. Eleven pounds, three ounces.
PONY: Ohhh, I want him, I want him!
WALLY: He's a great baby.

A silence as they all gaze at William.

FLETCHER *(Touches William's head and signs)*: He will be a leader of men.

PALACE: He says William will be a leader of men.

FLETCHER *(Signs)*: Your son was born under a highly elegant and aristocratic confluence of the planets.

Palace translates. Everyone gapes at Fletcher.

FLETCHER *(Signs)*: Because he was born on the seventh day of the seventh month, he's a totally evolved Cancerian who'll operate in large social dimensions.

Palace translates.

RANDY: Oh William, listen . . . !

FLETCHER *(Signs)*: His whole being cries out for the common good.

Palace translates.

FLETCHER *(Signs)*: He'll not only lead, he'll also create — forging bold new philosophies of tolerance and trust.

Palace translates.

RANDY: You hear that, William?

FLETCHER *(His signing gets more and more expansive)*: Like a precious jewel flung into a pond, his imprint will shiver and reverberate long after he's gone.

Palace translates.

FLETCHER *(Signs with foreboding)*: But be warned . . .

Palace translates.

CHARLOTTE: Oh no . . .

RANDY: What, what?

FLETCHER *(Signs)*: He will have to pay a price for these gifts . . .

Palace translates.

WALLY: I knew it!

CHARLOTTE *(Hands over her ears)*: I can't listen.

RANDY: What, what? Tell me!

FLETCHER *(Signs)*: His natal moon is in Scorpio, the demon sign . . .

Palace translates.

FLETCHER *(Signs)*: Just as he moves to better mankind, the scorpion's poison will flood his senses . . .

Palace translates.

RANDY: Stop, stop!

FLETCHER *(Signs)*: He'll be racked with jealousy and desire . . .

Palace translates.

RANDY: Please!

FLETCHER *(Signs)*: But all is not lost . . .

Palace translates.

FLETCHER *(Signs)*: Because of your son's fortunate trine aspect, he will vanquish the powers of darkness and walk in eternal light.

Palace translates. Silence.

RANDY: Did you hear that, William? You're going to be

a great man. I knew it, I knew it! *(He covers him with kisses)*

CHARLOTTE: Ohh, that was amazing, just amazing!

TURNER: How does he know all that?

PALACE: Fletcher's a psychic. He can read destinies through any medium . . . astrology, cards, palms . . .

PONY *(Pulling on Charlotte's arm)*: Oh, have another baby, Mommy. Have another baby!

RANDY: It's the way he expressed it.

PALACE: Yes, Fletcher's quite a boy. *(She signs to him)* They're all very impressed with you.

PONY: It would be so fun.

TURNER: Yeah, have another.

RANDY *(Puts William back in his carrier)*: Well, William, we'd better make tracks or Mom will be calling the ranger station.

PONY *(Pulling on Charlotte)*: Please?

TURNER: Please?

RANDY *(Shakes Palace's hand)*: It was a pleasure meeting you folks, and as for your grandson here, he's real special, real special! *(He squeezes Fletcher's arm, then waves to the Blossoms)* Be good. *(And he's gone)*

PONY: We'd help you take care of it.

CHARLOTTE: What's all this about having babies all of a sudden?

TURNER: Come on . . .

PONY: Ohhh, maybe it would be twins!

TURNER: Or triplets!

WALLY: Hey, hey, give your poor mother a break here.

PONY: Oh triplets! Go for it Mommy!

CHARLOTTE *(Laughing)*: Please!

PALACE: I had five myself. *(She signs to Fletcher)* Her kids want her to have more babies.

FLETCHER *(Signs)*: Babies are great.

PALACE *(Speaking and signing at the same time)*: Babies *are* great, but they're a lot of work. *(To the others)* There are long stretches of time I have absolutely no memory of.

PONY: It would be so neat. Babies in the kitchen, babies in the hall, babies rolling down the stairs . . . *(Clinging to Charlotte)* Goo goo, gaa gaa . . . goo goo, gaa gaa *(Etc.)*

TURNER *(Likewise)*: Babies in the yard, babies pouring out of the faucets . . . waa waa, waa waa *(Etc.)*

WALLY: Come on kids, cool it.

CHARLOTTE: I'm afraid it's too late.

PALACE: It's never too late. My mother had me when she was forty-seven. She didn't even know she was pregnant. She thought she had the flu.

PONY: Please? Pretty please?

CHARLOTTE: I can't.

PALACE: Who says you can't?

WALLY: Her body says she can't.

Charlotte breaks away from them.

PALACE: Oh, I'm so sorry.

Signing, she leads Fletcher away.

PALACE: Come on, sweetheart, I'll explain later.

PONY: What's wrong with Mommy?

Charlotte weeps and weeps.

TURNER: Mom, are you okay?

CHARLOTTE: Oh Wally, I can't bear it . . . I'll never feel life moving inside me again . . .

WALLY *(Arms around the kids)*: Hey, hey, you've still got Turner and Pony . . .

CHARLOTTE *(Racked)*: No, no, you don't understand . . .

WALLY *(Not moving)*: Honey, honey . . .

CHARLOTTE: It's like . . . like part of me's dying . . . . The best part.

SCENE 4

Wally and Turner are fly-fishing side by side in a mountain stream in Asheville, North Carolina. It's late afternoon the next day. Wally's wearing beat-up old hip boots and his fishing hat. Turner's barefoot in shorts and a light jacket. A liquid calm prevails.

WALLY: This is heaven . . . heaven!

TURNER: You said it.

WALLY: No one here except you and me. *(Pause)* And of course the fish.

TURNER: Fish are great.

WALLY: Fish *are* great! *(He casts)* Boom!

TURNER: They're so weird! What are they, anyway?

WALLY: Souls. Departed human souls.

TURNER: Come on . . .

WALLY: We begin life in water, so it's where we end up.

TURNER: Where did you get that? *(He casts with too much force)*

WALLY: Common sense. Our souls have to go somewhere. Oceans and streams are the only place left with any room, so they turn into fish. No, no, just flick your wrist like this. *(He demonstrates)* See? Flick!

Turner does a sloppy repeat.

WALLY: Don't *throw* it out. Just toss it out. It's all in the wrist. *(He demonstrates again)* Flick . . . flick . . . flick!

TURNER: Wait a minute, are you saying that all those trout darting around down there were once people?

WALLY: You got it. *(He casts again)* See that?

TURNER: That we'll be cooking up some bank robber or dead housewife for dinner?

WALLY: I hardly moved my arm at all. Bank robber, Indian brave, Joan of Arc . . . it could be anyone.

TURNER: And that I'm going to end up as a guppy or goldfish? That I'll spend all eternity swimming around in some kid's grimy fishtank . . . ?

WALLY: Not necessarily . . . you could get lucky and end up as a swordfish or twelve-ton tuna swimming off the coast of Bali. And it's not forever. You keep changing species . . . stingray one year, smallmouth bass the next . . .

TURNER *(Casts so violently he accidentally throws his pole into the water)*: Whoops!

WALLY: JESUS, TURNER!

TURNER *(Scrambles to pick it up)*: Sorry, sorry . . .

WALLY: I SAID: DON'T THROW IT!

TURNER: I'm sorry.

WALLY *(Reaching it first)*: That's a two-hundred-dollar rod and reel you've got there!

TURNER: I'm really sorry.

WALLY *(Wipes it off)*: Son of a bitch! *(A silence as he inspects it)* Well, you were lucky this time.

TURNER: It just flew out of my hands.

WALLY *(Handing it back to him)*: Okay, here you go.

TURNER *(Doesn't take it)*: No, I think I'll just watch.

WALLY: Come on, take it.

TURNER: I like watching you.

WALLY *(Forcing it on him)*: Will you take it?!

TURNER: Okay, okay . . .

WALLY: I've finally got a chance to teach you something I'm really good at, so take advantage of it!

TURNER: Okay.

Silence.

WALLY: I happen to be an ace when it comes to fly-fishing.

TURNER: I know.

Silence.

WALLY: So pay attention.

TURNER: Okay, I'm with you.

WALLY *(Picking up his rod again)*: It's like making music. The whole thing is to stay loose. *(He casts)* See that?

TURNER: Nice!

WALLY: Boom!

TURNER: Very nice, Dad.

WALLY: Just put it right out there!

TURNER *(Prepares to cast)*: All right fish: say your prayers.

WALLY: And . . .

TURNER *(Casts much better)*: Boom!

WALLY: Yes!

TURNER: I did it!

WALLY: It's all about the fine art of letting go.

TURNER *(Reeling in the line)*: This is fun.

WALLY: It's like when I was writing *The Atlantic Suite*. I could do no wrong. The melodies just kept coming. Adagios and obbligatos unfurled all around me. Cadenzas shivered overhead, fanfares swelled underfoot . . . . I wrote them down as fast as I could. It was amazing. Incredible! *(He casts again)* Boom!

TURNER: Or my spring recital at Juilliard. I was in a trance. It was so weird, I had the feeling my fingers had turned into a flock of parakeets or canaries . . . . I kept expecting to see all these feathers floating out over the audience. *(He makes eerie sound effects then casts beautifully)*

WALLY: Then pouf, it was all over. Granddad and Mamie both got sick, I was put in charge, and ashes, ashes, we all fall down. Though I can't blame everything on them. I just lost it, that's all. It can happen to anyone. The trick is to accept it and go down gracefully, right old buddy? Blub, blub, blub . . . *(Casts too vehemently and gets the line tangled)* Whoops!

TURNER: Hey, I think I got it!

WALLY *(Struggling to untangle it)*: Shit!

TURNER: Watch, Dad!

WALLY: Goddamnit!

TURNER *(Casts perfectly)*: Boom!

WALLY *(Making a worse and worse mess of it)*: What's wrong with this fucking line?

TURNER: Did you see that?

WALLY: I knew that guy sold me the wrong weight!

TURNER: Dad . . . ?

WALLY: Stupid asshole!

TURNER: I can do it now.

WALLY: You can do *what*?

TURNER: Cast.

WALLY: Well, any idiot can cast if they have the right line!

TURNER: Want to see?

WALLY *(Doubled up over his reel)*: Do you believe this?!

TURNER *(Casts perfectly)*: And . . . boom!

WALLY *(Tearing the line off the reel)*: We drive thirty miles to go fishing in this great secluded mountain stream and what happens . . . ? The goddamned line breaks on me! . . . *Unbelievable!*

TURNER *(Offering him his rod)*: Here, use mine.

WALLY: I don't want yours.

TURNER: Come on, take it . . .

WALLY: I said: *I don't want it!*

TURNER: But you were doing great.

WALLY: No, *you* were the one that was doing great, not me.

TURNER *(Trying to press it on him)*: Come on, Dad . . .

WALLY *(Pulls his line every which way, then finally flings his

rod into the water): Oh fuck it! Just fuck the whole
   goddamned thing!
TURNER *(Offering his rod again, eyes filling with tears)*:
   Dad . . . ?!

SCENE 5

*Midnight, two days and seventy miles later. The Blossoms'
tent is nestled in a moonlit clearing high up in the Smoky
Mountains. Everyone's asleep except for Charlotte, who's
sitting stock still, straining to hear something. It's pitch
black and eerie woodland sounds abound. A baby suddenly
cries.*

CHARLOTTE *(In a whisper)*: Wally . . . ? *Wally?*
WALLY *(Half asleep)*: Uuuhhhh . . .
CHARLOTTE: Listen!
WALLY: Uuuhhhh . . .
CHARLOTTE: There it is again.

*The crying stops and then resumes, sounding less and less
like a baby.*

CHARLOTTE *(Getting out of her sleeping bag)*: It's the baby.
WALLY *(Waking up)*: Hey, where are you going?
CHARLOTTE: He's been crying all night.
WALLY *(Grabbing her arm, amorous)*: I was just dreaming
   about you.
CHARLOTTE: I'll be right back.
WALLY: Hey, hey, not so fast! *(He tries to pull her into his
   sleeping bag)*
CHARLOTTE *(Resists, laughing)*: Honey . . . ?!

WALLY: Come here.

CHARLOTTE: What are you doing?

WALLY: Trying to get you into my sleeping bag.

The crying becomes more and more catlike.

CHARLOTTE: Wait! . . . Listen!

WALLY: Sweetheart, it's a stray cat! *(Nuzzling against her)* Mmmm, you smell so good!

CHARLOTTE *(Resisting)*: Wally . . . ?!

WALLY *(Pulling her into his bag)*: Come on, get in here. I never get to be alone with you anymore.

Thuds and crashes as he tries to haul her in.

CHARLOTTE: Honey, there isn't room . . . ! Gosh, you're right, that does sound like a cat!

WALLY: Mmmmm, you're so warm! *(A crash)* Whoops!

CHARLOTTE: Shhh! You'll wake the kids.

WALLY *(Trying to pull off her top)*: Come on, let's get this off. *(He accidentally pokes her in the eye)*

CHARLOTTE: Ow!

WALLY: Sorry, sorry . . .

CHARLOTTE: You hit me in the eye.

WALLY: I'm sorry. There. Is that better?

CHARLOTTE *(She starts to giggle)*: I don't believe this!

WALLY: Here, lift up a little.

Pony moans in her sleep.

CHARLOTTE *(Sitting up like a bolt)*: What was that?

WALLY *(Trying to get at her legs)*: What have you got on here?

CHARLOTTE: Shhh!

WALLY: Hiking boots?

CHARLOTTE *(In a whisper)*: Turner, is that you?

WALLY: Since when did you start wearing hiking boots to
bed? *(He drops one to the floor)*

Pony moans again.

CHARLOTTE: Turner . . . ?

WALLY: Goddamned sweatpants! *(He gets them off)* Ahhh,
this is more like it!

CHARLOTTE: Take off your shirt.

WALLY: Talk to me, talk to me.

*They embrace, laughing and groaning. Pony moans
again.*

CHARLOTTE: Honey, we're waking up the kids.

WALLY: Fuck the kids!

CHARLOTTE: WALLY?!

WALLY: What do you think families did in the old days
when everybody slept in one room?

CHARLOTTE: This isn't the old days.

WALLY: Our Founding Fathers didn't have separate
bedrooms and look how well they turned out!
Mmmm, you're so soft! I'd forgotten how soft you
were!

CHARLOTTE *(Trying to break away)*: I just can't in front of
them . . .

Wally croons with pleasure.

PONY *(Whimpering in her sleep)*: Stop, stop! I didn't do it,
I didn't do it!

Charlotte struggles to get out of the bag.

WALLY: Hey, where are you going?

PONY: No, no . . . put it down . . . . Melinda's in the kitchen with the ocean player.

CHARLOTTE: Turner's having a nightmare.

WALLY: Kids have nightmares. And that isn't Turner, it's Pony. *(Getting out of his sleeping bag, pulling her with him)* Come on, let's get out of here!

CHARLOTTE: Wallace . . . ?!

WALLY: Let's take a walk.

CHARLOTTE: But what about the kids?

PONY: Eeewwwww, there's a spider, look out, look out!

WALLY: They're asleep.

CHARLOTTE: And what if they wake up?

WALLY: They won't.

CHARLOTTE: How do you know?

WALLY: Because they never wake up in the middle of the night.

CHARLOTTE: Wally, you've lost your mind!

WALLY *(Grabbing her arm)*: Come on, let's go.

CHARLOTTE: Honey, you don't leave two small children alone in the middle of the Smoky Mountains!

WALLY: Don't we have any rights around here?

CHARLOTTE: I don't believe this!

WALLY *(Getting madder and madder)*: I mean, isn't this our vacation too?

CHARLOTTE: Shhh shhh, not so loud!

WALLY: What about us for a change? You and me?

CHARLOTTE: Oh God . . . !

WALLY: You only care about them!

CHARLOTTE: That isn't true.

WALLY: It is so! It's always the kids this, the kids that . . .

CHARLOTTE (*Trying to hush him*): Honey, please . . . ?!

WALLY: See what I mean? (*Heading for the door*) Look, you can stay chained to them if you want, but I'm taking a walk!

CHARLOTTE (*Following him to the door*): Wally . . . ?

WALLY: I don't even care if you come with me or not. (*And he's gone*)

CHARLOTTE: Honey, please! Now what do I do . . . ? (*She lurches back and forth between the door and the sleeping kids*) Oh shit! (*Then grabs a blanket and flashlight and rushes to the door*) Wally, wait up . . . ! (*Running back to the kids*) Please God, don't wake up . . . . Just . . . don't! (*And she's gone*)

A long silence, then spooky sounds start up. Wings flap, the baby cries and cries, an albino bat gives birth to kittens. Pony moans in her sleep. A lion roars close by.

PONY (*Wakes like a shot*): What was that?

Silence. Then all the sounds combine into a terrifying cacophony.

PONY (*In a whisper*): Mommy?

The sounds get louder.

PONY: *Mommy . . . ?!*

And louder.

PONY (*Frozen*): It's bears!

Dead silence.

PONY: MOOOOOOOOOOOOOOMYYYYYY???!
TURNER *(Wakes instantly)*: What's happening?
PONY: It's bears. Big black bears!

Silence.

TURNER: I don't hear anything.

The lion roars again.

TURNER *(Whispering)*: Dad . . . ?
PONY *(Whispering)*: Mommy . . . ?
TURNER: Is that you?
PONY: Can I get in with you?
TURNER: It's so dark in here.
PONY *(Creeping out of her sleeping bag)*: Where are you?
TURNER *(Likewise)*: Who has the flashlight?
PONY: Mommy . . . ?
TURNER *(Running into Pony)*: Dad . . . ?
PONY: No, it's me, Pony.
TURNER: *Pony . . . ?*
PONY: What?
TURNER: Oh no!
PONY: *Turner . . . ?*
TURNER: Where are they?

Silence.

TURNER: DAD . . . ?   PONY: MOMMY? . . .
    DADDY . . . ?   MOMMMYYYYYYY?

Silence.

PONY: *The bears got them, the bears got them!*

TURNER: Will you shut up?

PONY: I want Mommy, I want Mommy!

TURNER: Come on, quiet down or they'll get us too!

An instant silence.

PONY *(Jumping)*: What was that?

TURNER: What was what?

PONY: *That!?*

TURNER: I didn't hear anything.

PONY: It sounded like snakes.

TURNER: Will you stop it?

PONY: It's snakes, it's snakes!

TURNER: Wait a minute, let me get my circus light.

He turns on one of those little fiberoptic flashlights they sell at circuses and starts waving it, drawing liquid circles in the air.

PONY: Oh neat! Let me try.

TURNER: Use your own.

PONY: I don't know where it is.

TURNER: Look in your sleeping bag. *(He keeps waving it)*

PONY: Hey, I found it, I found it! *(She turns it on and copies Turner)* This is fun.

TURNER: I wish we had sparklers.

PONY: Oh, sparklers would be great!

They wave away until the tent starts to glow.

PONY: Hey, why don't you play your guitar.

TURNER: Now?

PONY: It would be neat.

TURNER: Yeah?

PONY: Yeah, we'll have a sound-and-light show. I'll do them both and you play that really beautiful piece . . .

TURNER *(With enthusiasm)*: Okaaay! *(He hands her his light and starts taking his guitar out of its case)*

PONY: Are you scared of seeing Livvie?

TURNER: Why should I be scared?

PONY: Because she's dying of cancer.

TURNER: So?

PONY: She'll look all strange. Her teeth will be black and she'll be wearing a wig.

TURNER: How do you know?

PONY: I heard Mommy and Daddy talking.

Turner starts playing Bach's Suite No. 1 in G Major. Pony listens for several measures, then resumes, waving the lights as Turner plays.

PONY: What if she dies in front of us? What if she turns blue and starts gasping for air . . . ? *(She makes lurid strangling sounds)* What if she wants to be alone with one of us? What if we're locked in the room with her and she comes after us . . . ? What if she falls and dies right on top of us . . . ?

There's a sudden awful noise outside.

PONY *(Dropping the lights)*: IT'S HER, IT'S HER . . . . SHE'S COMING TO GET US!

Turner continues playing.

PONY: HELP . . . HELP . . . !

TURNER *(Stops playing)*: Jeez, Pony!

PONY: She's coming to get us, she's coming to get us!

TURNER: She lives over two thousand miles away!

PONY: Mommy, Mommy . . . !

TURNER *(Rising)*: I'm getting out of here, you're crazy!

PONY: Hey, where are you going?

TURNER *(Heading for the door)*: I want to see what's going on.

PONY: You can't go out there.

TURNER: Who says?

PONY: The bears will get you! *(In a frantic whisper)* Turner . . . ?!

TURNER *(Pulls back the tent flap and steps outside)*: Ohhh, look at all those stars!

Moonlight pours through the door.

PONY: Turner, get back in here!

TURNER: The sky's full of shooting stars. Quick, Pone, you've got to see this!

PONY *(Whimpering)*: I want Mommy, I want Mommy . . .

TURNER *(Returning for Pony)*: They're amazing. Come on, give me your hand.

PONY: Where are we going?

TURNER: Just follow me.

He leads her to a clearing outside the tent. The sky is ablaze with shooting stars.

TURNER *(Putting his arm around her shoulder)*: Well, what do you think?

PONY: Ohhhhh, look!

TURNER: Isn't it incredible?

PONY: Look at all those stars!

TURNER *(Pointing)*: Oh, one's falling, one's falling!

PONY: There are millions of them . . .

TURNER: Did you see that?

PONY: . . . billions and zillions of them!

TURNER: Come on, let's get closer.

PONY: Ohhh, they're so bright!

Arms around each other, they walk deeper into the starlit night.

TURNER: Hold on tight now. I don't want to lose you.

The curtain slowly falls.

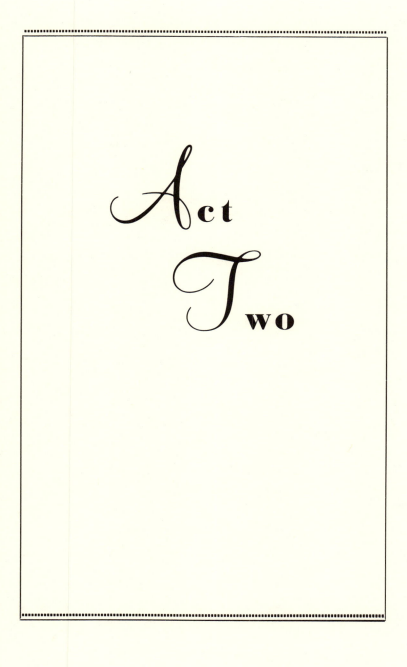

Act Two

SCENE 1

It's four days and seven hundred miles later. The Blossoms are in a sailboat scudding across a lake in Oklahoma City with Charlotte's brother, Scotty Childs; Joy, his new wife, who's black and seven months pregnant; and Amy, his daughter from his first marriage. Amy's at the tiller wearing a Little League shirt and cap. She looks suspiciously like a boy. The grownups are drinking champagne and laughing. Pony's sitting close to Joy waiting to feel the baby move, and Turner's sunbathing on the deck. The wind slaps against the sails as they skim over the water. It's one of those idyllic summer days you remember for a lifetime.

SCOTTY (*Laughing*): Wait, wait, there's more . . .

JOY: You and Charlotte packed a fourteen-inch cast-iron frying pan . . . ?

SCOTTY: . . . a fourteen-inch cast-iron frying pan, an orange-juice squeezer, an electric toaster . . .

JOY: But Scotty, how did it all fit in a doll's trunk?

ALL *(Roaring with laughter)*: *It didn't!*

CHARLOTTE: *Plus* . . .

WALLY: Plus a gallon of milk, a bottle of maple syrup . . .

TURNER: Three jars of peanut butter . . .

PONY: Four-and-a-half bananas . . .

AMY: Five bags of marshmallows . . .

CHARLOTTE: And Horatio, my life-size pink teddy bear!

JOY *(Laughing)*: Stop, stop . . . !

WALLY *(Hopping up with his camera)*: Nobody move! I've got to get a picture of this! *(He starts snapping away)*

SCOTTY: And of course . . . the crucial carton of eggs.

CHARLOTTE: Yes, don't forget the eggs.

TURNER, PONY AND AMY: The eggs, the eggs, the eggs!

WALLY *(Snapping away)*: OH YES!

CHARLOTTE: Which all smashed when I tried to shut the lid.

AMY: *Yuck!*

PONY: Eeewy gooey, eeewy gooey.

JOY: This is the saddest story I've ever heard.

SCOTTY: What do you mean?

CHARLOTTE: It's not sad.

JOY: Running away from home to fry eggs on top of a mountain . . . ?

SCOTTY: We were city kids. *(Tilting the champagne bottle)* A little refill, Char?

CHARLOTTE: We wanted to join Livvie out West. She'd built herself this canvas dome high up in the Tetons. It was the shape and color of a giant apricot. It was that crazy dome that inspired Scotty to move out here and become a landscape architect. *(Holding out her glass)* Please!

SCOTTY *(Pouring)*: It's true. I still remember the pictures of it. It was a cross between a hot-air balloon and a mad scientist's observatory . . .

WALLY *(Taking more pictures)*: What a day . . . ! It's days like this that make you feel you can do anything.

CHARLOTTE: She wanted to be close to the sky . . .

WALLY: Swim the Atlantic, ride bareback on a zebra, write music that will leave audiences sobbing in their seats. It's all just . . . *out there,* swaying within reach.

CHARLOTTE: This was in her painting days before she moved to the desert . . . which she says is even closer to the sky.

WALLY: The thing is to seize it! *(He roars with resolve)*

JOY: I understand wanting to run away to join her . . .

WALLY: Thrust out your arms and partake!

JOY: But to fry eggs . . . ?

SCOTTY: She made great eggs. *(Lifting the bottle towards Wally)* Wallace?

CHARLOTTE: She made *great* eggs!

WALLY: Please! *(Extending his glass)*

Scotty fills it.

JOY: When I ran away from home, it was to CBS in Chicago because I wanted to be a newscaster so badly.

CHARLOTTE: You were just more realistic, that's all. *(Mopping her brow)* Gosh, it's hot out here!

JOY: The only problem was, it was over five hundred miles away, and it took me four days to get there.

WALLY *(Drinks in great gulps)*: Crawl out of your hole and partake!

CHARLOTTE: But look how it paid off! I mean, here you are interviewing kings and presidents all over the place.

JOY *(Jumps, hand over her stomach)*: WHOA!

PONY: I felt it, I felt it! *(She presses her head against Joy's stomach)* Again, again!

CHARLOTTE: Our dream was to make it out West and fry eggs with wild-and-woolly Livvie . . . *(She fans herself)*

SCOTTY: We would have walked across Siberia to be with her.

WALLY *(Flings his head back and closes his eyes)*: Ahhhh!

CHARLOTTE *(With affection)*: Look at Wally . . . ! *(Taking his hand)* Having fun, sweetheart?

WALLY: This is the life.

Charlotte leans against him and sighs happily.

WALLY: Everything is music. All you have to do is listen.

PONY *(Pressing her head into Joy's stomach)*: Neato! I can hear it breathing. *(She breathes loudly)*

JOY: *Her,* not it! She's a girl. Your mommy wove her the most amazing quilt covered with dragonflies . . .

PONY: It's a girl? How do you know it's a girl?

JOY: Because I had a special test. Really Charlotte, you could show your things in art galleries . . .

WALLY: That's what I keep saying.

JOY: They're so beautiful.

CHARLOTTE: Please! It's just a hobby.

PONY: What kind of a test?

JOY: A test where they take out some of the fluid the baby is living in.

PONY: Ewwwww, ewwwwwww!

JOY: It doesn't hurt.

CHARLOTTE *(Quietly to Scotty, shifting away from Wally)*: So, when did you see Livvie last?

SCOTTY: Amy and I flew up two weeks ago. She's becoming quite a little pilot.

CHARLOTTE: You go all the way to Taos in the Cessna?

SCOTTY: It's a snap. With favorable winds we can make it in three hours.

JOY: Babies live in special sacs filled with water.

CHARLOTTE: And how was she?

SCOTTY: Not good.

WALLY *(To Charlotte)*: Come back, come back.

PONY: Then how do they breathe?

JOY: Through gills. They start out like fish.

AMY: Ewwwww . . . ewwwww!

CHARLOTTE: Yeah, she sounded pretty rocky on the phone the other day.

SCOTTY *(Voice lowered)*: It's just a matter of days.

CHARLOTTE *(Hands over her ears)*: Don't . . .

SCOTTY: You'll make it in time, don't worry.

CHARLOTTE: Oh Scotty . . . !

SCOTTY: I know, I know. *(He takes her hand)*

CHARLOTTE: Well, racing to finish "The Ring of Prayer"

in 102-degree heat didn't help. Sybil was furious with her.

SCOTTY: What would we do without that woman? She's not only a great doctor, but she and Sinclair are the only ones Livvie will listen to.

CHARLOTTE: I don't know which I dread more — getting there too late or having to see her suffer.

SCOTTY: The worst is over, it's just a matter of letting go.

CHARLOTTE: Stop . . .

JOY *(To Pony)*: You see, nature is very logical. Since life began in water, we begin in water too. When a baby's tiny it looks just like a fish. Then it grows hair and lungs and turns into an egg-bearing mammal . . .

PONY: Wow . . . !   AMY: Gee . . . !

PONY: You mean, *I* was a fish?

JOY: We all were! *(She makes fish faces and laughs)*

PONY *(Yelling over)*: HEY TURNER, DID YOU KNOW WE ALL STARTED OUT AS FISH?

TURNER: No, we *end up* as fish, silly.

A silence.

SCOTTY: Hey, Amy, how about giving someone else a turn?

AMY: Sure, anyone want to sail?

PONY *(Raising her hand)*: Oh me, me!

SCOTTY: Turner?

TURNER: I don't know how.

AMY: Come on, I'll teach you. It's easy.

SCOTTY: She's an ace, she's been sailing since she was two. Go on, give it a whirl.

Turner joins her.

PONY *(Softly to Charlotte)*: Amy is so weird. Are you sure she's not a boy?

CHARLOTTE: Now Pony . . .

AMY *(Showing Turner)*: This is the tiller. It's like a steering wheel, except you move it in the opposite direction you want to go. *(She moves it from side to side)* See? It's a cinch.

JOY: The girl's amazing. She's captain of the track team, she plays first base for Little League, and don't ask me where this came from—but she's a crackerjack at archery!

CHARLOTTE: Well look at her mother . . .

SCOTTY: You look at her!

WALLY: What's old Inge up to these days?

AMY *(Handing over the tiller)*: Now you try.

SCOTTY: Running marathons, if you can believe it.

PONY: Mommy . . . ?

WALLY: You're kidding.

SCOTTY: She's gone off to Calcutta to train.

WALLY: Calcutta?

JOY: No, no, Kenya. He mixes them up on purpose.

SCOTTY: So, to continue our saga . . .

PONY: Mommy . . . ?

JOY: Yes, do, do!

CHARLOTTE: It just gets worse, believe me.

WALLY: Hey, Turn, how're you doing?

TURNER: Great!

AMY: He's a natural!

PONY: *Mommy?!*

WALLY AND CHARLOTTE *(Angry)*: What is it, Pony?

PONY: This is fun.

SCOTTY: Good girl! That's just what I like to hear . . .
(He tousles her hair) So, after Char smashed the eggs
trying to close the doll's trunk, we realized we had
too much stuff. We decided not to bring anything.

PONY *(Snuggling up to Joy again)*: You're so pretty.

JOY: Why thank you, honey.

PONY: I love your hair. *(She starts playing with it)*

JOY: Ugh, you can have it! *(To the others)* What I can't
get over is that your parents let you go.

CHARLOTTE: They were very liberal.

JOY: If I lived in New York City and Amy suddenly
announced she was going to run away from home to
fry eggs on top of the Tetons, I wouldn't let her out
the door!

SCOTTY: Well, there were two of us, remember.

JOY: But you were only eight and eleven . . .

PONY *(Still involved with Joy's hair)*: Can I brush it?

JOY: . . . you were just babies! *(Starts rummaging around
in her bag)* Sure, I think I've got a brush in here
someplace . . .

TURNER: LOOK EVERYBODY, I'M SAILING, I'M
SAILING!

CHARLOTTE *(Waving to him)*: Yay Turner . . . !

AMY: Tomorrow I'm going to teach him how to windsurf.
That's *really* fun!

WALLY *(Getting out his camera and taking more pictures)*:

Wait'll they see this back at Juilliard . . . Turner at the helm. And suddenly he's surrounded by a herd of killer whales.

AMY (*Pointing into the distance*): Thar she blows!

JOY (*Finds a brush and gives it to Pony*): Here you go.

PONY (*Brushing away*): Ohhh, it's so curly! I wish I had hair like this!

JOY (*With disgust*): Please!

AMY (*Grabbing Turner*): Look out, look out, one's right underneath us! Man the lifeboats! (*She starts running up and down*)

AMY AND TURNER: MAN THE LIFEBOATS! MAN THE LIFEBOATS!

SCOTTY: Easy Amy, easy. (*Pause*) So . . . we announced our plans on a bright Sunday morning in April. Father said it was fine with him, and he gave us a couple of dimes in case we wanted to call from the road. Mother just warned us not to talk to strangers . . .

JOY (*To Scotty*): Incredible!

CHARLOTTE (*Fanning herself*): And never to accept anything from them.

JOY (*Noticing Charlotte's discomfort*): Hey, are you okay?

CHARLOTTE: Particularly soda. (*To Joy*) It's this brutal Oklahoma sun.

SCOTTY: She said wicked people sometimes pour poison in it when you're not looking so they can rob you. She then told us to be back by 1:30 for lunch because . . . (*A weighty pause*)

SCOTTY AND CHARLOTTE: "We're having chocolate sundaes for dessert!"

CHARLOTTE: Oh Scotty, I wish you didn't live so far away!

SCOTTY *(Reaching for it)*: Hey, how about another bottle of champagne?

WALLY *(Putting his camera away)*: Sounds good to me! *(He suddenly starts humming the woodwind section of a melody that's come to him)*

SCOTTY *(Uncorking the bottle as he talks)*: We headed into Central Park, figuring that was the best place to start looking for mountains.

CHARLOTTE: I would have followed him anywhere, *anywhere!*

JOY *(To Pony)*: Would you like me to brush *your* hair? It's so pretty. It shines like corn silk.

PONY: Sure!

JOY: My little sister and I used to do this for hours . . . . Hours! *(She brushes Pony's hair into a series of fancy styles)*

SCOTTY: And before we knew it, we were standing in front of the lion's cage at the zoo. *(Lifting the bottle in Charlotte's direction)* Char?

CHARLOTTE: Please!

SCOTTY *(Fills her glass, then moves towards Wally)*: Maestro?

WALLY: Let 'er rip! *(He keeps humming his melody)*

Charlotte starts sprinkling herself with drops of champagne.

SCOTTY *(Pouring)*: That's my man! If you come up with some new quartet or symphony on this boat, *I* expect some of the credit now . . .

WALLY: You got it. *(Tilts his glass to him and drinks)* Ahhhhh . . .

JOY *(To Pony)*: How about we sweep it all on top of your head and make you look like a princess?

PONY: Ohhh, that feels so good. Isn't Joy beautiful, Mommy?

CHARLOTTE *(Guiltily stops dousing herself)*: Very.

JOY: Please! I'm a blimp!

CHARLOTTE: In fact, Joy's one of the most beautiful women I know.

SCOTTY: Here, here . . . . So, there we were watching the lion pace back and forth when this man suddenly comes up to us and says, "You children aren't out here all alone, are you?"

JOY: Oh God . . . !

CHARLOTTE: Naturally we don't answer him since Mother told us not to talk to strangers . . . *(She pours more champagne into her glass)*

SCOTTY: But then he looks really concerned and asks, "Have you lost your mother and father . . . ?"

JOY *(Sceptical)*: Right, right . . .

CHARLOTTE: No, he seems genuinely concerned, so we say, "No, we're running away from home."

JOY: Oh no!

SCOTTY: So *he* says, "You're running away from home, are you? Where are you going?"

JOY: I can't listen to this!

CHARLOTTE: So, *we* say, "To the top of a mountain to fry eggs with Livvie!" *(To Scotty)* We really *were* crazy, you know. *(She dunks her hand in her glass and sprinkles more champagne over herself)*

SCOTTY: And *he* says, "Gosh, that sounds like fun. Can I come with you?"

JOY: Stop . . .

CHARLOTTE: So we say, "Sure." *(Pause)* This is really great champagne.

JOY: These things really scare me.

WALLY *(Draining his glass)*: This *is* great champagne!

SCOTTY *(Handing him the bottle)*: Help yourself, I've got lots more on board . . .

WALLY *(Refills his glass)*: Ahhh, just what the doctor ordered . . . . You were absolutely right Char, this has turned out to be a terrific trip, really terrific! *(He lets out a roar and tilts the bottle Charlotte's way)* How about some more?

CHARLOTTE: Thanks . . . . So, there we are telling this guy about all our plans while the lion keeps pacing back and forth in his cage . . . *(She douses her arms and shoulders directly from the bottle)*

SCOTTY: We're going on and on about how we're going to hook up with our crazy Aunt Livvie who paints twelve-foot canvases of clouds and sky, when he suddenly says, "You know, we're standing in a very vulnerable spot in relation to this lion because of the wall behind us. If he suddenly decides to take a leak, it's going to hit the wall and ricochet all over us like a loose fire hose."

JOY: Scotty, this is getting weird.

SCOTTY: The guy then launches into this lecture about the great force with which lions pee, and how the wall behind us will just act as a conductor. So Char and I start to get a little nervous. I mean, this is *not* the sort of conversation we're used to . . .

Charlotte is now pouring the champagne all over herself.

SCOTTY: When all of a sudden, the lion looks us straight in the eye, lifts his leg, and lets fly the most horrendous piss you've ever seen! We are talking broken water main here . . . . It comes streaking past us at ninety miles an hour, slams into the wall just as the guy predicted and—SPPPPLATTTTTT!— we are drenched! I mean, soaked from head to foot!

JOY *(Laughing)*: Oh no.

CHARLOTTE *(Pouring the champagne over her head)*: It was unbelievable!

WALLY: *Honey . . . ?!*

SCOTTY: Charlotte, what are you doing?

A silence as they all stare at her.

CHARLOTTE *(Guiltily hides the bottle behind her)*: Oh, sorry, sorry . . . I was a little hot.

WALLY: Then you go in for a swim. You don't waste good champagne.

SCOTTY: Hey, how often do I get to see my little sister?

CHARLOTTE *(Mopping herself off)*: Sorry, this is a new thing with me. It's like I'm on fire all the time.

WALLY: Jesus.

JOY: That's some story . . . !

SCOTTY: It's not over yet.

JOY: Oh no.

SCOTTY: We made it back to the apartment just as Mother was filling our milk glasses.

JOY *(Laughing)*: I don't believe a word of this.

CHARLOTTE: Father took one look at us and said, "Good Lord, what happened to you on top of that mountain? It looks as if a lion peed all over you!"

She and Scotty roar with laughter.

JOY: He followed you.

CHARLOTTE *(Still laughing)*: He followed us.

WALLY: It's such a wonderful story.

SCOTTY: Father worked in mysterious ways.

CHARLOTTE: You can say that again. *(Pause)* We had a great childhood.

SCOTTY: A great childhood!

CHARLOTTE: The best.

WALLY *(To Turner)*: HEY SKIPPER, HOW'S THE WHALE SITUATION?

TURNER: We scared them all away.

WALLY: That's my boy! Just look at him. The kid can do anything, anything! *(He roars with pride)*

TURNER: Let's us get a boat!

CHARLOTTE: Oh, Turner, Turner . . . . Why do I love little boys named Turner so much?

JOY *(Has finished Pony's hairdo)*: There, you're done. You're one beautiful little girl, you know that? *(She gives her a big kiss)*

PONY *(Prancing up and down)*: Look at me, look at me!

SCENE 2

Early evening, two days and 230 miles later. Turner and Pony come running out of the Panhandle Diner thirty miles east of Amarillo, Texas. They head for the car, Pony pretending she's Wally, and Turner pretending he's Charlotte.

PONY *(Sliding behind the wheel)*: COME ON GUYS, GET A WIGGLE ON!

TURNER *(Gets in next to her)*: It would be nice to reach a campsite before dark for once!

PONY *(Yelling out her window)*: KIDS . . . ? *(To Turner)* What's your cash situation like?

TURNER *(Yelling out his window)*: LET'S GET MOVING! *(To Pony)* Eighty-five cents.

PONY: Great, that's just great! I have a dollar fifty! *(Pretends to turn on the ignition)* Well, let's just hope we've got enough gas to make it to Armadillo.

TURNER: Amarillo, *Amarillo!*

PONY: Jesus, Char, what are those kids up to? We paid the check ten minutes ago. *(Yelling out the window)* PONY . . . ?!

TURNER: TURNER . . . ?!

PONY *(Softly)*: What do you say we take off without them?

TURNER: Now you're talking! Come on, step on the gas!

PONY *(Making accelerating sounds)*: Those kids are history!

Charlotte and Wally come streaming out of the diner—Charlotte pretending she's Turner and Wally pretending he's Pony.

WALLY: Mommy, Mommy, Mommy . . . ?!

CHARLOTTE *(Getting into the car behind Turner)*: They're leaving without us!

WALLY *(Clambering in next to her)*: Mommy, Mommy, Mommy . . . !

PONY: Shit!

TURNER: They caught up with us.

PONY: Just our luck!

TURNER *(Turning around, all smiles)*: Hi kids.

PONY: Son of a bitch!

WALLY: No fair, Turner's in my seat!

CHARLOTTE: I am not!

WALLY: You are so!

CHARLOTTE: Am not!

WALLY *(Starts pounding on Charlotte)*: Give me my seat back!

CHARLOTTE *(Hitting back)*: Cut it out, Pony!

WALLY: OW, OW, TURNER'S HITTING ME, TURNER'S HITTING ME!

TURNER: Careful of his hands now . . . . Come on Wally, *do* something! I can't take this anymore.

Charlotte and Wally keep slugging each other.

PONY: *You* can't take it . . . ? What about me? I'm having a fucking nervous breakdown!

WALLY: You're so mean, you're so mean . . . OW . . . OW . . . . No fair!	CHARLOTTE: I'm going to kill you, Pony, I really mean it!

It escalates.

TURNER: KIDS, KIDS . . . . ENOUGH IS ENOUGH!	PONY: IF YOU DON'T STOP IT RIGHT THIS MINUTE, I'M GETTING OUT OF THE CAR!

PONY: THAT'S IT . . . ! WE'RE TURNING
AROUND AND GOING BACK HOME!

TURNER: Sweetheart?

PONY: This vacation is over!

WALLY: I'm sorry, we'll be good, we'll be good.

PONY: It's too late.

TURNER: But what about Livvie?

WALLY: Daddy's mad. I hate it when Daddy's mad.

PONY: Livvie, Livvie . . . everything's always Livvie.
You're on the goddamned phone with her every other
day!

CHARLOTTE: Don't worry, he'll get over it.

TURNER: I had another one of my dreams last night. I
finally found the baby I keep hearing crying outside
the tent.

PONY: Oh no, not another one of your crazy dreams!

TURNER: I picked him up and brought him inside to
show you.

WALLY: I've got to pee.

CHARLOTTE: So do I!

TURNER: And he was enormous! So big I could hardly
carry him.

WALLY: *Mommy?!*

TURNER: Except it wasn't a baby and it wasn't a boy.

CHARLOTTE: We've got to pee!

PONY: Easy kids, easy . . .

TURNER: It was Livvie. She'd been buried alive . . .

WALLY AND CHARLOTTE: We've got to pee, we've got to
pee, we've got to pee!

PONY: Buried alive . . . ? *(Whirling around)* I said: CAN
IT!

They do.

PONY: Thank you. *(To Turner)* And . . . ?

TURNER: She was all covered with mud and leaves and
stuff and she was roaring with laughter, saying
"Hubba-hubba, hubba-hubba." Shaking and
sputtering, with tears rolling down her face, saying
it over and over again. "Hubba-hubba, hubba-hubba,
hubba-hubba!" *(Pause)* It was terrifying.

WALLY: I miss Spit and Wheat Germ!

WALLY AND CHARLOTTE *(In a loud wail)*: Spitty, Spitty,
Spitty, Spit!

PONY *(Under her breath)*: This is a fucking madhouse!

TURNER *(Softly)*: Wally, I *wish* you wouldn't use that kind
of language in front of them!

PONY: I mean, after a while . . .

WALLY: Mommy . . . ?

TURNER *(Fanning himself)*: Jeez, it's hot in here!

PONY: . . . how much can a guy take?

CHARLOTTE: Dad, can I move up front with you?

WALLY: Mommy?

PONY *(To Charlotte)*: No, you can't move up front with
me!

TURNER *(Taking off his shirt)*: I don't know about the rest
of you, but I'm burning up!

CHARLOTTE: Please?

PONY: I said, no!

Turner starts fanning his naked chest.

WALLY: Mommy . . . ?

PONY *(To Turner)*: Charlotte, what *are* you doing?

TURNER: I'm hot!

WALLY: *Mommy . . . ?!*

TURNER AND PONY: WHAT IS IT, PONY?

WALLY: This is fun! *(He grabs a candy bar out of Charlotte's pocket)* Nyah, nyah, I've got your candy bar. Anyone want some?

CHARLOTTE *(Trying to snatch it back)*: Hey, that's mine!

They start fighting.

CHARLOTTE: Ow, ow, watch my hands . . . ! *(She lifts them up and examines them)* Jeez, Pony!

PONY *(Suddenly gets out of the car, slamming the door behind her)*: I CAN'T TAKE THIS ANYMORE, YOU DRIVE!

TURNER: Honey . . . ?

CHARLOTTE *(Starting to get out)*: Great! Now I can sit up front!

WALLY *(Pulling her back)*: Oh no you don't! It's *my* turn to sit up front! *(Starts slugging her)* TURNERRRR?!

They fall into another fight.

PONY *(Storms to the back of the car and gets in behind the driver's seat, pushing Wally over and Charlotte out)*: MOVE!

CHARLOTTE *(Falling with a crash)*: OW!

WALLY: Daddy, what are you doing?

CHARLOTTE *(Dashes over to Turner's door and starts pushing him towards the driver's seat)*: Move over, Mom! *(Back to Wally)* Nyah nyah, I got here first!

TURNER *(Being pushed behind the wheel)*: Turner . . . ?!

WALLY *(Storms out the backseat after Charlotte)*: Oh no you don't . . .! *(And gets into the front seat, shoving Charlotte behind the wheel and Turner out onto the ground)*

TURNER: Hey . . . ? What's going on?

CHARLOTTE: Jeez, Pony!

WALLY: No fair, no fair!

PONY: This is more like it, now I have the whole backseat to myself!

TURNER *(Comes around to the back and pushes Pony over)*: That's what you think! Move over!

Turner slams his door, Wally slams his, Pony slams hers and Charlotte slams hers.

CHARLOTTE *(To Wally)*: Hi Pone.

WALLY *(To Charlotte)*: Hi Turn.

PONY: GREAT IDEA! LET THE KIDS DRIVE!

TURNER *(Stunned)*: What?

CHARLOTTE *(Turning on the ignition)*: Far out!

WALLY: Go for it, Turner!

TURNER *(To Pony)*: They can't drive!

PONY: Who says?

TURNER: Honey, you've lost your mind.

PONY: I don't know why we didn't think of this before. It solves everything!

CHARLOTTE *(Gunning the gas pedal)*: And . . . we're off!

SCENE 3

Taos, New Mexico, two days later, around noon. The Blossoms have just been ushered into Olivia Childs' bedroom by Dalia Paz, her Mexican nurse. Pony clings to

Charlotte's shirt, terrified. Turner's next to her, carrying his guitar. Olivia's fourposter bed dominates the room. It's shrouded with masses of fabric, making it look like a gauze cathedral about to lift off the ground. A vase of orchids sits on her bedside table and an oxygen hookup is nearby.

DALIA: Come . . . she is expecting you. *(She sweeps across the room and lifts the gauze around the bed; to Olivia)* Ya llegaron, Señora. [They are here, Señora.]

Olivia doesn't stir.

DALIA: She sleeps and sleeps. *(Waving them closer)* Please . . .

Wally and Charlotte gingerly step forward.

PONY *(Being pulled with them)*: No, no, no, no . . .
CHARLOTTE *(Taking Olivia's hand)*: Livvie . . . ? Livvie? It's me, Charlotte.

Pony keeps whimpering.

DALIA: Your family is here, Señora. Wake up, wake up. They want to see you.
CHARLOTTE *(Softly)*: How are you feeling?
DALIA *(To Olivia)*: Vamos, abre los ojos. Han venido de muy lejos. [Come, open your eyes. They have traveled a long way.]
CHARLOTTE: That's all right, let her sleep.
DALIA: No, no she sleeps too much. Despiertate, despiertate! Estas muy caprichosa! [Wake up, wake up! You're being very naughty!]
CHARLOTTE: We can come back later.

DALIA *(Angry to Olivia)*: Asi es como te vas a comportar cuando tu familia te viene a visitar? [Is this how you behave when your family comes to see you?]

Nothing.

PONY: She's dead, she's dead!

CHARLOTTE:	WALLY: Can it,	TURNER: God,
PONY . . . ?!	Pony, just can	Pony!
	it!	

CHARLOTTE *(To Dalia)*: She's too young to understand.

DALIA *(Not understanding)*: Please?

CHARLOTTE: I said . . . she doesn't understand.

Dalia looks at her blankly.

CHARLOTTE *(Embarrassed)*: She thinks she's dead.

DALIA *(Upset)*: Oh no, no, Señora! She is not dead! Don't say such things. She is sleeping.

CHARLOTTE: I know, I know . . .

DALIA *(Mimes sleeping for Pony)*: She is sleeping.

CHARLOTTE *(Voice lowered)*: She's too young to understand, she's just a baby.

DALIA: Yes, she sleeps like a baby. She's my little angel. *(She strokes Olivia's forehead and murmurs)* Y en dónde estas ahora, mi querida? Nadando en una playa azul como un pescadito, o volando más alto que las nubes como una grande aguila? [And where are you now, my precious one? Swimming in the clear blue ocean like a little fish? Or flying high above the clouds like a great eagle?]

Silence as the Blossoms stare at the floor.

DALIA *(Noticing Turner's guitar)*: You play the guitar?

TURNER: Yes.

DALIA: I play too.

TURNER: Yeah?

DALIA *(All modesty)*: Just a little.

TURNER: That's great.

DALIA: Not great just . . . so-so . . .

TURNER: Come on, I'll bet you're really good.

DALIA *(Blushing)*: No, no . . .

WALLY: Play for us!

TURNER: Yes, do! *(He hands her his guitar)* Come on . . .

CHARLOTTE: We'd love to hear you.

DALIA *(Stroking it)*: What a beautiful guitar.

CHARLOTTE: And it might help wake her up.

DALIA: It's been so long, so long . . . I used to play and dance in the hills . . .

She bends over it, takes a deep breath and starts playing and singing a spectacular flamenco song complete with hand slapping and Gypsy yelps. The Blossoms stare at her, open-mouthed, then gradually thaw, snapping their fingers and tapping their feet. Wally suddenly starts to dance. Charlotte joins him in a torchy duet. Then the kids join in, feigning a bullfight. They get more and more carried away.

DALIA *(Finishes in an inspired burst and hands the guitar to Pony)*: Gracias.

The Blossoms break into wild applause.

TURNER *(Staring at Dalia)*: That was amazing!

WALLY: Spectacular!

Olivia moans.

DALIA: She's awake! *(She goes over to her)* Señora, ellos
llegaron. [Señora, they are here.]

OLIVIA *(Groggy)*: Music . . . I heard music.

DALIA *(Propping Olivia up)*: Anda, anda . . . . Abre tus
ojos. [Up, up . . . . Open your eyes.]

*Olivia is raised to a sitting position. She's terribly old and
frail, to the point of transparency. She opens her misty eyes.
The Blossoms gasp.*

PONY *(In a whisper)*: She's alive!

*Olivia abruptly shuts her eyes and sinks back into her
pillows.*

TURNER *(To Pony)*: Now look at what you did.

PONY *(Terrified)*: I'm sorry, I'm sorry . . .

CHARLOTTE: Oh Wally, I didn't think she'd be this bad.

DALIA *(Pulling her back up)*: Señora, no sea caprichosa.
Quieren verte. Han venido de muy lejos. [Señora,
don't be naughty, they want to see you. They've come
a long way.] Open your eyes!

Olivia opens her eyes and looks around blankly.

DALIA: See? They're here!

OLIVIA *(To Dalia)*: Who are these people?

CHARLOTTE *(Leaning over her)*: It's me, *Charlotte!*

DALIA: Your family, my angel!

CHARLOTTE *(Taking her hand)*: Oh Livvie, it's so good to
see you again. You look wonderful.

OLIVIA *(Peering at Charlotte)*: Scotty?

CHARLOTTE: No, it's me, *Charlotte*. Scotty's in Oklahoma City.

WALLY: You look great!

CHARLOTTE: Doesn't she?

OLIVIA *(Suddenly spies Turner)*: Amy!

CHARLOTTE: No, no, this is Turner.

OLIVIA *(Stretching out a bony arm)*: Amy, Amy, come closer and let me get a good look at you.

Pony whimpers in terror.

CHARLOTTE: Livvie, it's me, *Charlotte*. This is my son, *Turner!*

OLIVIA *(Gesturing more frantically)*: Closer, I can't see you!

PONY *(Clutching on to Wally)*: Daddy, Daddy . . . !

CHARLOTTE *(Shepherding them closer)*: Come on kids, you're too far away . . .

WALLY *(Pulling her forward)*: Pony . . . ?!

PONY *(Digging in her heels)*: No, no, no . . .

CHARLOTTE *(To Olivia)*: See, it's me, Charlotte, and here are my two children, Turner and Pony . . .

OLIVIA *(Snatches Turner's hand)*: Amy . . . ! Come, give your poor old great-aunt a kiss like a good little girl. *(She makes lurid kissing noises)*

Turner freezes and Pony whimpers.

OLIVIA: Don't be frightened, I won't bite.

Turner leans over and gives her a quick peck on the cheek. Pony's whimpering gets louder.

WALLY *(Under his breath)*: Stop it, Pony! Just . . . stop it!

OLIVIA *(Gazing at Turner)*: I can't get over how much she looks like a boy.

CHARLOTTE *(Getting the giggles)*: Oh God . . .

OLIVIA: Why do you cut her hair so short and dress her this way?

DALIA: Señora, this *is* a boy!

WALLY *(Under his breath, referring to Dalia)*: Obviously she hasn't met Amy!

He and the kids start to giggle.

CHARLOTTE *(Chastisingly)*: Wally!

OLIVIA *(Pulling Turner closer)*: You're such a pretty little girl. Why don't you let your hair grow?

CHARLOTTE: Livvie, this is my son, *Turner!* He's going to play for you later.

OLIVIA: Ah yes, you play baseball, don't you?

The Blossoms' giggles increase.

TURNER: Come on, guys . . .

PONY *(Swinging Turner's guitar)*: Batter up . . . . Play ball!

OLIVIA *(Notices Pony for the first time)*: And who is this?

TURNER: My sister.

OLIVIA *(Seeing her with the guitar)*: So you were the one playing the music just now . . .

DALIA: That was me.

TURNER: No, I'm the one that plays.

OLIVIA: I didn't know you had a sister that played the guitar. Well, well . . .

DALIA: No Señora, *I* was playing . . . *(To the others)* She gets confused sometimes.

OLIVIA *(To Pony)*: You play very well.

PONY: Thank you.

> *Olivia suddenly falls back into her pillows, eyes closed, mouth open. Silence.*

CHARLOTTE: Maybe we ought to let her rest awhile, I'm afraid we're tiring her out.

WALLY: Good idea.

CHARLOTTE *(Starts moving towards the door, voice lowered)*: Come on kids, we'll come back later.

DALIA *(Fussing over Olivia)*: Duerme, mi ángel. Volveran. [Sleep my angel. They'll be back.]

WALLY *(Herding the kids towards the door)*: Quietly, quietly . . .

PONY: Shhhhhhhhh . . .

CHARLOTTE *(Whispering to Dalia)*: We'll see her after lunch.

DALIA *(Crooning to Olivia)*: Descansa, mi querida. Vuelve a tus sueños. [Rest, my sweet one. Go back to your dreams.]

> *The Blossoms start tiptoeing out the door. Olivia suddenly sits up, thrusting out an arm.*

OLIVIA *(In an agonizing cry)*: NO, NO, DON'T GO! DON'T LEAVE ME!

SCENE 4

> *Later that evening, around nine. A bedside lamp glows eerily in Olivia's room. She's being examined by her doctor,*

Sybil Wren, a hearty woman in her sixties who has a severe limp. Wally, Charlotte and Dalia stand nervously in the doorway. Turner and Pony are spread out in the hall playing Hearts.

SYBIL *(Stethoscope on Olivia's chest)*: All right now, take a deep breath.

She takes a shallow one.

SYBIL: Hold it.

She does.

SYBIL: Okay, you can let it out.

She does.

SYBIL: Again.

They go through it again.

SYBIL: Good. Now cough.

She coughs weakly.

SYBIL: Again.

And weaker still.

SYBIL: And once more.

It's barely audible.

SYBIL: Oh Liv, what are we going to do with this poor tired-out old body of yours?

OLIVIA *(In another world)*: No, no, just back up the truck over by the canyon . . .

SYBIL: How's the pain?

OLIVIA *(Agitated)*: Why would I bring candles? The shovel's under the porch! OW, OW . . . STOP IT! THAT HURTS!

SYBIL: I know, I know . . .

OLIVIA: STOP IT, YOU'RE CRUSHING MY CHEST! *(She whimpers)*

Sybil kisses Olivia's brow, puts away her stethoscope, snaps her bag shut.

SYBIL *(To the others)*: I almost thought she'd lick it.

CHARLOTTE *(Leaning against Wally, weepy)*: I can't bear it, I just can't . . .

WALLY: Oh honey . . .

SYBIL: She's such a crafty old bird.

Dalia lurches out of the room with her hands over her face.

CHARLOTTE *(Suddenly breaks away, weeping)*: Oh Wally, it all goes so fast . . .

SYBIL: She's always got one more trick up her sleeve.

WALLY: Honey . . . ?

CHARLOTTE: I'm sorry, I'm sorry, I just can't keep up . . .

SYBIL *(To Olivia)*: Come on, show us your stuff.

CHARLOTTE: You dance through childhood, race through the teenage years, fall in love a couple of million times, bear some delicious bald babies, and then . . . whhhhhhst, it's all over . . . . Don't you ever feel like digging in your heels and shouting, "SLOW DOWN GUYS AND LET ME GET THE LAY OF THE LAND FOR A MINUTE!" . . . *(She pauses and*

looks around the room) It's nine o'clock in the evening
. . . the children are playing cards in the hall . . .
there's a sweet smell in the air. What is it?
Pistachios! The whole room smells of pistachios
. . . ! Livvie's sleeping with her mouth open. Look
at her. Poor thing, she looks like an old man . . . .
Just slow down and take it all in . . . . Sybil's
wearing silver earrings, Wally's got a bruise on his
arm, someone's heart is beating like crazy . . . .
Shhh! Listen! . . . Lub dub, lub dub, lub dub, lub
dub . . . . It's *my* heart! Nobody move . . . . The
moment's holding . . . . *(In a whisper)* It's perfect
. . . perfect . . . !

A silence.

OLIVIA *(Babbling)*: The children are in the meadow flying
kites . . . . There's Franklin in his pinafore. Wait for
me . . . wait for me . . . !

SYBIL: It's funny, I've been feeling real anger lately . . .

CHARLOTTE: Oh, Wally . . . !

SYBIL: I keep thinking about that first project I went on
with Liv when I lost my leg. You know, her eight-
mile highway of sails that wound around Chaco
Canyon. The reason I lost it was because she was so
intent that they all fly at precisely the same height.
And that was no small task when you consider she
used over three thousand sails rigged on forty-foot
masts . . . . It was beautiful as hell, but back-
breaking work. We were a crew of 150 . . .

OLIVIA *(Overlapping)*: Come on Franklin, it's my turn

. . . . Oh no, Boxer's loose, Boxer's loose! Bad dog, go back to Mummy!

SYBIL: I was rehoisting the last one five-and-a-half inches higher, and she just serenely backs the truck over me . . . I mean, here I take off time from medical school to help her on the project, and she runs over my leg for five-and-a-half lousy inches. Do you believe it?

OLIVIA: Wait, wait, I've got a stone in my shoe . . .

SYBIL: Well, the woman has me bewitched, I'd follow her anywhere. It's just lately I've been feeling this deep resentment. I mean, it's hard enough being a female doctor out here, but then to be a one-legged one on top of it . . .

CHARLOTTE AND WALLY: Sybil . . . !

Turner and Pony suddenly appear at the door.

CHARLOTTE: Oh, hi, kids!

A pause.

SYBIL: I'm not complaining, I'm not complaining. I have a wonderful life. Sinclair's a great husband and we have two fabulous children . . . . It's just there's so much more I wanted to do.

Turner and Pony edge over towards Wally.

WALLY: Yeah, I know what you mean. Our feelings play strange tricks on us. *(Putting an arm around each)* Oh, hi guys. This has been a tough year. The last thing I wanted to do was drive to New Mexico to watch another relative die. But the closer we got, the better

I began to feel. I mean, look at us . . . we drove
over two thousand miles and we're still talking to
each other. We had a few laughs and saw some
dynamite scenery. It was a great trip, a great trip!
And here's poor Livvie hanging on by a thread, and
I'm still raring to go. Charlotte's in another world,
the kids are terrified, and you're furious . . .

PONY *(Gazing up at him)*: Hi Daddy.

WALLY: Hi Pone, what's happening?

OLIVIA *(Moaning in her sleep)*: Amy, Amy, I want to see
Amy . . .

CHARLOTTE: What's she saying?

OLIVIA *(Garbled)*: The little girl who played the
music . . .

WALLY: I think she wants to see Turner again.

OLIVIA *(Beckoning towards the kids)*: Closer . . . come
closer!

WALLY: Go on Turner, she's calling you.

Turner starts to approach her.

OLIVIA: No, the other one. Bring me the other one.

CHARLOTTE *(Nodding in Pony's direction)*: Her?

WALLY: Pony?

TURNER: My sister?

OLIVIA *(Pointing directly at her)*: THAT ONE! The little
girl with the glasses!

They all stare at Pony, who goes rigid.

WALLY: Well, Pone, I guess you're the one she wants this
time.

PONY *(Frozen, barely audible)*: No, no, no, no . . .

SYBIL: Don't be afraid, she won't hurt you. *(Pushing Pony towards her)*

WALLY: Come on, Pone, there's nothing to be afraid of.

CHARLOTTE: Honey, she just wants to look at you.

PONY *(In a frantic whisper)*: Turner, you promised you wouldn't leave me alone with her . . . *Turner . . . ?!*

WALLY: Atta girl . . .

CHARLOTTE: Honey, you're embarrassing us!

SYBIL: I was the same way at her age, exactly the same . . .

Olivia starts to chuckle in a terrifying way.

PONY *(Eyes closed)*: She'll die on me, she'll die on me . . .

CHARLOTTE *(Horrified)*: PONY . . . ?

PONY: HELLLLLLLLLLP!

Turner looks on helplessly.

OLIVIA *(Sounding more and more like a witch)*: Yes, *she's* the one I want . . .

PONY *(Flinging her arms around him)*: SAVE ME, TURNER . . . SAVE ME!

Wally and Charlotte pry her away.

TURNER: I'm sorry Pone, I'm sorry . . .

SYBIL: Don't be scared, she's gentle as a lamb . . .

Charlotte drags Pony, head bowed and eyes closed, to Olivia's bedside. A long silence as Olivia glares at her. No one breathes. Olivia suddenly stages a little show. She bleats like a lamb, howls like a coyote and crows like a

rooster. She then rips off her wig, revealing a bald pate.
Everyone screams. Dalia comes running into the room. Dead
silence.

OLIVIA: I just wanted to make sure you were paying
attention.

SYBIL: Typical, typical.

DALIA *(Crossing herself)*: Santa María de la Cruz!

CHARLOTTE: Livvie!

WALLY: Whoa! You nearly gave me a heart attack!

Olivia then pulls off her bald pate, revealing a crop of
sparse white hair which she coyly fluffs into place.

TURNER *(Starts applauding her)*: Wow! Way to go!

PONY: That was really neat!

OLIVIA: There, this is more like it.

SYBIL: See what I have to deal with? You can't trust her
for a minute.

OLIVIA: Now there's a little life around here!

PONY: Again, again!

SYBIL *(To Olivia)*: And here we were practically
administering last rites. You are very naughty!

OLIVIA: Well, a dying old lady's got to have some fun.

PONY: More, more!

CHARLOTTE: You're too much, too much!

PONY: Gee, you're really neat!

OLIVIA *(Sighs deeply and shuts her eyes)*: All right, now
everybody leave the room.

DALIA *(Protesting)*: Señora . . . ?!

OLIVIA *(Pointing a stern finger)*: I said, go!

DALIA: But someone has to stay with you.

OLIVIA: You heard me. I want to be alone.

SYBIL *(In a whisper, moving towards the door)*: Come on, we'll wait outside the door.

OLIVIA *(Highly agitated)*: GO, GO, GO!

SYBIL *(Shepherding them all out)*: All right, all right.

They all tiptoe towards the door.

OLIVIA *(Pointing at Pony)*: Except for her! I want the little girl to stay.

PONY *(Amazed)*: Me . . . ? You want *me?*

OLIVIA: Yes. You stay!

PONY *(Happy)*: All right!

Everyone stares at Pony.

PONY: You heard her, we want to be alone.

SYBIL *(Starting to move)*: Okay okay, but if you need us, we'll be right outside.

DALIA: What about changing your bedclothes?

OLIVIA: *I said GO!* And shut the door behind you.

PONY: Yes, shut the door behind you.

Everyone leaves. Dalia shuts the door. A silence.

OLIVIA *(Closes her eyes, then opens them and smiles)*: There, this is more like it. Sit down, sit down.

Pony pulls up a chair next to her and sits.

OLIVIA *(Casually plucks an orchid out of her vase and starts eating it)*: Mmmmm . . .

Pony watches, amazed.

OLIVIA: Would you like to try one?

PONY: Could I?

OLIVIA *(Handing it to her)*: Please!

PONY *(Takes a cautious bite)*: Mmmm, I've never had this kind before. *(She eats with rising gusto)*

OLIVIA: They're orchids.

PONY *(Finishing it off)*: It's so sweet!

OLIVIA: An old admirer sends them to me from Hawaii. Here, have some more.

She hands Pony a few and takes more herself. They munch away, smiling at each other and wiping their mouths.

PONY *(Between swallows)*: How old are you?

OLIVIA: Eighty-one.

PONY: *Eighty-one . . . ?* Gosh, that's so old!

OLIVIA: And how old are you?

PONY: Nine.

OLIVIA: *Nine . . . ?* Is that all? I thought you were thirteen or fourteen . . .

PONY: No, just nine.

OLIVIA: I'm amazed!

PONY: When's your birthday?

OLIVIA: July 7th.

PONY: Oh, that's right. We just met a baby that was born on the same day. He was so cute. *(Pause)* What's your favorite color?

OLIVIA: White. And yours?

PONY: Blue.

OLIVIA: Blue's all right.

PONY: And what's your favorite animal?

OLIVIA: The snowy owl. And yours?

PONY: *Horses!*

OLIVIA: Horses. Of course!

PONY: Do you have a lucky number?

OLIVIA: One.

PONY: *One?* That's so weird.

OLIVIA: What's yours?

PONY: Four.

OLIVIA: How come?

PONY: I don't know, it just is.

Silence.

OLIVIA: I like your glasses. Could I try them on?

PONY: Sure. *(She takes them off and hands them to her)*

OLIVIA *(Putting them on)*: Ohhhh, these are great!
Everything's so clear!

A silence as she gazes around the room.

PONY: How do you go to the bathroom if you have to
stay in bed all day?

OLIVIA: In a bedpan.

PONY: What's that?

OLIVIA: A kind of portable toilet. Would you like to see
it?

PONY *(Thrilled)*: *Could I?!*

OLIVIA: Sure. *(She whips it out from under the covers and
holds it aloft)* What do you think?

PONY: Oh, that's neat!

OLIVIA *(Handing it to her)*: Here, sit on it, it's like a little
throne.

PONY *(Puts it on the seat of her chair and sits on
it)*: Wow . . . ! *(She makes a peeing sound)*
Psssssss . . .

OLIVIA *(Offers her the first wig she had on)*: Now put this on for the full effect . . .

PONY *(Puts it on and tucks her hair inside)*: Psssssss psssssss . . .

OLIVIA *(Starts laughing and clapping her hands)*: Perfect, perfect! *(She suddenly has a seizure and grabs for the oxygen mask)* Air . . . air . . . *(She gropes wildly to get it on)* Help me, I can't get it on, I can't get it on . . .

PONY *(Rises and gropes for the unit)*: Wait, I can't see . . .

OLIVIA: Air . . . air!

> *She finally gets it on. Her breathing becomes more labored. She takes several more deep breaths and is restored. She removes the mask and hangs it up. She gazes at Pony and smiles. A silence.*

PONY: What happened?

> *Olivia shuts her eyes and sighs.*

PONY: Are you okay?

OLIVIA *(Drifting off to another world)*: Come, let's move into the shade. I don't like all these bees.

PONY: I thought you were dying.

OLIVIA *(Waving her hands at the invisible bees)*: Shooo shoo . . .

PONY: Death is so scary. Aren't you scared? I don't want to die.

> *Olivia keeps shooing away the bees.*

PONY: I get so scared thinking about it, I can't sleep. Every night I touch my bedside light forty-four times and hold my breath for as long as I can and pray, *"Please God, don't let me die! I'll be good, I'll be good!"* And then I start imagining what it will be like . . . . You know, being dead in a coffin, being underground all alone in the dark . . .

OLIVIA: What's that smell? I know, it's cloves . . . . Cloves!

PONY: . . . with mice and, and spiders, and worms crawling over me . . . and, and dead people moaning all around me . . . and trying to call Mommy and Daddy but they can't hear me because I'm so far underground . . .

Olivia breathes heavily.

PONY *(Getting more and more upset)*: And, and then I start thinking about being there forever and ever and ever and ever until my body's a skeleton . . . a clattery skeleton with grinning teeth and no eyes, and I touch my night-light 144 times so it will go away, and then 244 times, and 444 times, and I get crying so hard Mommy has to come in and hold me . . . . And, and . . . . Oh no, it's starting to happen now . . . . Could I get in bed with you? *(Climbs in next to her, whimpering)* I don't want to die, I don't want to die . . .

OLIVIA *(Waking, groggy)*: I just had the most beautiful dream . . .

PONY *(Clinging to her)*: Hold me, hold me!

OLIVIA: No, it was a reverie because it actually happened. Yes . . . it happened a long long time ago.

PONY: Tighter!

OLIVIA: I was on a train . . . *(She reaches for a nasal cannula that feeds her more oxygen)* Wait, just let me put this on, it helps me remember. *(Still in Pony's glasses, she puts it on)*

PONY *(Reaching out for her)*: Hold me!

OLIVIA *(Breathing easily)*: Ahhh, that's better, much better . . . I was on a train . . .

PONY *(Burying her head in Olivia, wig still on)*: I don't want to die, I don't want to die!

OLIVIA *(Putting her arms around her)*: There, there, no one's going to die . . . . I was on this horrid train on my way to the Sahara Desert . . . . Yes, there was something about the Sahara Desert back then . . . . I wanted to get lost in it, fling myself face down in it . . . . I'd been studying painting in Paris for the year. How could I have forgotten . . . ? I was all of twenty. Mercy, this was a thousand years ago. During my wild days. *(She roars)* What I put my poor parents through! Well, you'll do it too, you'll do it all, just wait and see . . . . Poor thing, you're shivering . . .

PONY *(Whimpering)*: I don't want to die, save me, save me!

OLIVIA: What's all this talk about dying all of a sudden? . . . I was on a train somewhere between Paris and Tangier . . . we'd stopped at some godforsaken town in the middle of nowhere, and standing on the platform was the most beautiful man I'd ever seen—tall, with olive skin and a thrilling mouth. He wore a white suit and was pacing up and down the platform carrying this enormous bouquet of poppies that stained his face crimson. I couldn't take my eyes off him. He was like something out of *The Arabian Nights.* I kept expecting to see peacocks and jeweled elephants stamping in the distance. Finally he caught my gaze . . . I pressed my face against the window and whispered, "My name is Callisto!" *(She laughs)* Do you believe it? I used to call myself Callisto in those days . . . . The train suddenly started up. We pulled out of the station. I watched him get smaller and smaller. Then I fell into a deep sleep. I began having nightmares . . . I was being chased down this long tunnel . . . I started to scream. Someone grabbed my hands. I opened my eyes. It was him! He'd jumped on the train at the last minute and was sitting across from me, eyes laughing, poppies blazing . . . . He didn't speak a word of any language I knew, but he held me spellbound. I never made it off the train. He wrapped me in his flying carpet and wouldn't let me go. You've never seen such feverish carryings-on . . . . He rocked me over mountains, sang me through rain forests and kissed me past ancient cities. Oh, what a ruckus we made! Well, you'll do it too, you'll do it all, wait and see. We ended up in Zanzibar, island of cloves. *(She removes her nasal cannula)* I was so full of him, I thought my heart would burst. Zanzibar! *(She starts to rise, reaching for Pony's hands)* Come on, jump with me . . .

PONY *(Taking her hands and bouncing)*: This is such a bouncy bed.

OLIVIA: It was there that he taught me how to live on

orchids and read the stars . . . . Zanzibar, say it!

PONY: Zanzibar! Hey, let's play Geography!

They start jumping together.

OLIVIA: We visited the wonders of the world without taking a step . . . Baghdad!

PONY: Detroit!

OLIVIA: Vienna!

PONY: Alabama!

OLIVIA: Nicosia . . .

PONY *(Stops jumping)*: No, no you're not playing right. Alabama ends with A, so you've got to name a place that starts with A!

OLIVIA: Addis Ababa! *(She resumes jumping)*

PONY: That's right! Arizona!

OLIVIA: Athens!

PONY: Sacramento!

They jump higher and higher.

OLIVIA: Oslo!

Dalia, Charlotte, Wally and Turner come bursting in. They skid to a stop when they see the two of them bouncing on the bed; Olivia still in Pony's glasses, Pony in Olivia's wig.

DALIA: Señora, Señora . . . ?

PONY: Ohio!

CHARLOTTE: Livvie?!

WALLY: What's happening?

OLIVIA: Odessa!

TURNER: Pony, what have you got on your head?

PONY: We're playing Geography! *(She rips off the wig and flings it in the air)*

OLIVIA: *Odessa!*

PONY: Albuquerque!

CHARLOTTE *(Starts laughing)*: It's a miracle, a miracle!

SYBIL *(Comes streaking in)*: Finally . . .

PONY: *Albuquerque!*

SYBIL *(Laughing)*: You see, you see . . . ?

OLIVIA: Egypt!

SYBIL: What did I tell you!

CHARLOTTE: Look at her go!

WALLY: Unbelievable!

TURNER: She's great, really great!

CHARLOTTE: Go Livvie!

WALLY: Jump!

OLIVIA: I said Egypt! What's the matter with you? Are you deaf?

PONY: Oh, sorry, sorry . . . um . . . Tallahassee!

OLIVIA: Equador!

PONY: Rhode Island!

WALLY: *Jump!*

OLIVIA *(Starts to weaken)*: Denmark.

PONY: Kansas!

OLIVIA *Weakening more)*: Shanghai!

SYBIL *(Easing Olivia down to the edge of the bed)*: Easy, easy . . .

OLIVIA: I said . . . Shanghai!

PONY: Islip! It's in Long Island.

OLIVIA: Paradise!

PONY: Paradise.

OLIVIA: Come on, say it loud and clear.

PONY: Paradise!

OLIVIA: Again!

PONY *(Bouncing higher)*: Paradise!

OLIVIA: And again!

Pony jumps higher and higher. She starts doing wondrous spins in midair.

PONY: Paradise . . . . Paradise . . . . Paradise!

ALL *(Massing around the bed, overlapping, continuous and euphoric)*: Paradise . . . Paradise . . . Paradise . . . Paradise . . . Paradise . . . Paradise . . . Paradise . . . *(Etc.)*

The light around Pony becomes more intense. Hair flying and nightie billowing, she looks like a reckless angel challenging the limits of heaven. The curtain slowly falls.